19 Days In March

ARTHUR AND JOYCE BECKER

Fulton Books
Meadville, PA

Published by Fulton Books 2022

ISBN 979-8-88505-181-1 (paperback)
ISBN 979-8-88505-182-8 (digital)

Printed in the United States of America

Chapter 1

Thank You

March 4, 2020

It was hazy. My mind tried to comprehend what was going on, but I couldn't focus mentally or physically. What the hell? I tried to open my eyes, but all I was seeing was a blur, like how I can't focus my eyes in a fog. I couldn't understand where I was. I couldn't see anything. The air felt warm, but whatever I was on had cold sheets and a cold metal bar. Finally—*finally*—I heard someone…I think.

"Mr. Becker? Mr. Becker, are you okay?"

"Uurrrggghhh." That was all I was able to get out. *What is wrong with me, man?*

"Artie? Artie, you're okay. You're out of surgery."

Oh, thank God, it was Joyce, my one true love—the one who has stayed beside me and supported me for over a decade and agreed to be my wife.

"Urrggghhh."

And then that was it. It was black again, and I was out.

*****

I was slowly shaken awake by the swaying of a seat. I was in a car. The sun was warming my head, and man, did I feel sick. I could focus a little better now and saw Joyce driving. We were going under the Cross Valley Expressway, but I was still lethargic, slow, and heavy.

I felt like I was wearing a suit of weights. I was struggling to open my eyelids and turn my head to her. I couldn't speak.

I could see Joyce with a hue around the outline of her features. Colorful. She was surrounded in a rainbow almost. Wow, she was beautiful. While driving, she did notice that I could see her. She smiled at me and reached her arm out.

"Thank you for doing this for us," she said, and she took her hand to clutched mine. Her hand and her voice were reassuring.

Slowly I remembered. I tried to smile, but it got dark again quickly. Aaand then I was out.

The next thing I remember with any kind of clarity was waking up on a couch. It was a little later in the afternoon; I could tell by the way the shadows were hitting the wall. It doesn't seem like anyone is around. I tried to move my legs around, and then that is when I felt a terrible pain between my legs that made me instantly scream out.

"Holy Moses, that hurts!" I exclaimed as I slowly tried to sit up. I heard little feet running across the floor from the kitchen, heading straight toward me. As she came around the corner, I saw it was Clara, our youngest daughter, running with an ice pack in her hands.

"Daddy! You okay?" she said as she tossed the ice pack on my leg. I took it and gently put it on my crotch.

"Thank you, hon!"

She then gave me a big hug.

"Daddy hurt?"

"Yeah, but I will be okay."

"Hey, you okay? I sent Clara in with the ice pack. Thought you might need it," Joyce asked as she walked in.

"Sore a lot and groggy. How long was I out?" I grabbed the ice pack and began to position it ever so gently.

"Well, do you remember anything?" she asked.

"Not really." The ice pack was helping with the pain. I still couldn't sit up, though.

"They brought me back to see you around noon. We left at one, and you woke up just now. It's a little before four," she said as she sat in her chair.

Everyone had their own chair, and I had the couch. Mom's chair was nice; it was a motorized reclining chair but was one and half the size of a normal chair. Usually, she was there with our two dogs: our dachshund Buddy and our cocker spaniel Shaggy.

"Are all the drugs wearing off?"

"Yeah, I can kind of focus now. It's just been all a blur. It does hurt to move my legs, but it's not terrible." The pain wasn't as bad as I thought it was going to be. Even only a few hours after the surgery, I expected constant agony or stabbing pain like I did when I had my gallbladder removed. This type of pain in the crotch was just slightly higher than tolerable—like I had been kicked by one of the kids really hard.

"Daddy had drugs?" asked little innocent Clara.

"Yes, Daddy had surgery, and they gave him drugs to go to sleep," said Joyce before I had a chance to respond. "Are you hungry?"

"Oh no, I am good for now. Maybe later. Did you take care of your mom's fire?" Joyce's mom, also named Joyce (though I call her Momma Joyce), lived next door to us. After we got married, we bought her parent's neighbor's house so that we could be close to them. Both of our houses were heated with coal, and usually, it was my job to take care of it. But given the circumstances right now, I've got a short vacation of two or so days.

"Yeah, I took care of that. I'm going to wait for Peanut on the bus," Joyce said as she got up and walked out of the room with Clara following behind her.

"Wait for me, Mom!" she shouted excitedly as she tried to fit her five-year-old little feet quickly into her shoes.

Peanut was our oldest daughter's nickname. Her name was also—wait for it—Joyce. Yep, my mother-in-law, my wife, and my first daughter were all named Joyce. That absolutely wasn't planned; that was just the way the dominoes of life fell into place with the most important women in my life. Peanut was her nickname because when she was born, she was such a tiny baby. Clara's nickname was "the Mayor." That was because when Clara was a baby, she used to come in the room and scream and cry at us at home, but in public, all she wanted to do was talk to everyone and be social, like a mayor.

Peanut was in the third grade, and her mom was a music teacher in the same school district. They weren't in the same building all the time, but throughout the week, my wife would have classes at my daughter's school. So they did get to see each other occasionally. I did like the fact that Joyce was a teacher; it made me feel better that she was close to them all the time.

I lay back down on the couch and could hear the traffic outside. I heard the normal sounds of the cars and the outside world, and after a brief few minutes, I could hear a large vehicle pull up to the front of the house. My youngest daughter started to squeal with delight. It was the bus, and I was sure that Peanut was sleeping in her seat, so someone was trying to wake her up right now. I couldn't blame her. The kid had a thirty-five-minute bus ride to and from school, so why not grab a quick nap?

As the bus pulled away, I could hear the kitchen door burst open with Clara and Peanut already fighting about something. Joyce calmed them both down and started to make dinner as Peanut walked up to me to give me a hug.

"Oh! Oh! Careful, hon!" I shouted as she was about to jump on top of me.

"Joyce! Your dad just got back from the doctor's. You can't jump on him for a few days, okay? You can give him a hug, though!" yelled back my wife as she was in the kitchen.

"Hi, Dad. You going to be okay?" asked Peanut as she put down her book bag to give me a hug. She leaned over me to give me a hug with her little arms and her little hands. So cute.

"Yeah, Daddy is going to be okay. How was school?"

"Math," she replied as she rustled through her book bag.

It's not that she hated math. She was very good at it, but it was her least liked subject. My wife and I always worked with her because it was not 100 percent her teacher's job to educate her. She needed us to be involved too.

She finished getting what she was looking for—her homework—and sat at the table to start it while her sister was at the table, playing on a tablet. Soon enough, Joyce was done making dinner, and while they all ate, I lay on the couch, trying to get comfortable, watching the news with the sound off.

The news had always been basically three things to my wife and me: how many houses burned down, how many car crashes there were, and what the weather is. After the weather report, we'd both kind of lose interest because unless it was hockey, we didn't pay attention to the sports segment. Over the past few weeks, though, something different had been getting more and more airtime. The Wuhan flu, the coronavirus, or COVID-19, whatever the hell it was, from where we were sitting looked like it could be something we should probably be paying more attention to.

They shut down the city of Wuhan, China. When the news announced that the city was on lockdown and showed pictures that the city was barren (like, no one was moving), that was when Joyce and I paid attention. We had to online map where the city was and saw that it was a huge city—like, a really big city. To shut it down and stop everything was probably a big deal, so Joyce began bringing in hand sanitizer to work and was being extra cautious around the kids. She didn't think that she'd get sick, but she knew all too well that schools could be like petri dishes, for God knows what, and this was something that, if it got loose in the schools, could be very bad.

After dinner and homework was done, Joyce came to join me in the living room while the girls went upstairs to play video games. There it was again on the news—the coronavirus.

"What is the virus doing this time?" she asked as she sat down.

"Well, China is still locked down and—*oh my god, look at that!*" I shouted at the screen. There were images of a British cruise ship, and right now, it was quarantined with 706 cases of the virus. To top it all off, they couldn't disembark any of the passengers where they were—Japan. They did not know when the passengers could leave or where the ship was going to go next. In the same segment, it flickered back and forth between Italy and a nursing home in Kirkland, Washington. My wife and I just looked at each other. What the heck was this thing?

"Could you imagine being in that nursing home?" Joyce asked as her attention turned back to the TV since the weather was about to come on.

"Looked like I picked a hell of a time to get a vasectomy," I joked as the phone rang. It was my sister. I picked up before the kids did because when they answer the phone, they just take off to some random part of the house and begin talking nonsense. I picked up the phone and put it on speaker so my wife and I could talk to her.

"Hey, fatty," said my sister in her way of endearing sisterly love.

"Hey, Bot." My sister's name was Elizabeth. But when she was little, she talked with a monotone voice, so we called her Robot, which shortened to Bot.

"So did you go to the courthouse to change your name? What did you pick? Artina or maybe Katlyn?"

"Liz, I keep telling you I did not have a sex change operation or gender reassignment. It was safer for me to get fixed over Joyce, and since we don't want more kids, I did it."

"You be nice to him, Liz," chimed in my wife as she smiled at me. "He did something very special for me, for us. Thank you again so much, Artie."

"Yeah, well, he is still fat and stupid. Now MBA stands for 'maybe balls absent,' Arty Becker, MBA."

When I first got my MBA degree, I would sign my name with MBA after it. I stopped it after a while because it seemed tacky or inappropriate for someone in the trucking industry. But my sister never lived it down.

"Ehhh, that's not that funny, Liz. Just stick to the master of branches," said Joyce as she started laughing.

When my sister and her ex-husband were over at our place two years ago to help me take a tree down, she started making fun of me explaining how I wanted the tree to come down. After that, MBA meant "master of branches."

"You know I am still in pain, right, everyone?" I asked quizzically.

"Oh, oh, oh, you had a few hours of surgery, and it's the end of the world. Your wife birthed two kids, one of them without an epidural, and you think you should get special treatment because you're in 'pain'? Ha! Listen, fatty, I am just calling to see how you are doing and if you told Mom yet."

Oh yeah, my mom was totally against me getting this done. She felt it should be Joyce who gets it done because she had it done. To her, it wasn't the man's job to have that done in the relationship.

"No, I did not tell Mom yet, and I will thank you not to tell her either," I said.

"Oooh boy, I can't wait to tell her. Talk to you later, Joyce, Arty. I love at least one of you," said my sister before she hung up.

"Ha! I bet she is going to tell your mom," said Joyce as she got up to go upstairs and check on the kids.

"God, I hope not. You're going to put the kids to bed tonight?" I asked as I pulled a blanket up over me.

"Yeah. Are you hungry yet?" asked Joyce.

"No, I think I am going to hobble up to bed and get on the machine."

I slept on a sleep apnea machine so that I wouldn't stop breathing in the middle of the night. I also legitimately wasn't hungry. The anesthesia was messing with my stomach, and I just was not in the mood.

"Okay, if I come in and you're sleeping, I will let you be."

"Thanks, beautiful. Hey, Joyce, did I have a chance to tell you today that I think you're the most beautiful woman in the world and that I am so happy that I married you?"

Ever since we started dating, I told her that almost every day, except back then, she was my girlfriend.

"I love you too, hon. You rest up."

March 6, 2020

The light was breaking through the window as I struggled to get my sleep apnea mask off my face. Joyce was already up and taking a shower. Two days of rest seemed to be all that I needed to recover from the surgery. The pain was gone, and it was just a dull ache, really. I was up early enough to get Peanut out of bed and ready for school, so that was one less thing that she needed to worry about. Peanut and I went downstairs to the kitchen as Joyce got done with her shower.

"Whoa, someone is doing better. How are you feeling, Artie?" asked Joyce, and she walked over to the refrigerator.

"Much better. I will put 'nut on the bus so it frees you up a bit," I said as I gave her a kiss on the cheek.

"Thanks. Is Clara up yet?" she asked just as we heard the *thud* above our heads—the distinct sound of that little girl as she hopped out of bed to run downstairs to us. "Yeah, I guess she is. Hey, while you are home today, do you want to call the arena to see if we can get tickets to Sunday's game? I got an email this morning that there is going to be a special for the afternoon game. The kids can each get a free ticket with the purchase of our adult tickets."

Thinking about it, we were almost through the season, being in March, and we had not gone to a single game. Ugh, I really didn't have the money for this. "Okay, sure. I will call up that guy who is always trying to sell me season tickets."

"Okay, and make sure you get seats that are only four in the row, like down by where the ice cleaning machine comes onto the rink."

"Got it. Anything else?" I asked her as I was getting Peanut out the door to the bus. Aaand of course, she had to chime in with something.

"Yeah, Mom, because you know that Dad does everything," said 'nut with an eight-year-old's smirk. What a pot stirrer she is! It was because one time on Christmas Eve, I may have said something under my breath which, while not those exact words, out of a moment of temporary duress, no one in this family would let me live down. Joyce just smiled back.

"That's right, he does do everything, doesn't he?"

"Ugh, oh my god. Once again, I did not say that. Thanks for tearing open that old scab, hon. Come on. Off to the bus with you."

With that, as I waited for the bus, Joyce got a head start on getting off for school—I meant work. I kept saying that. For my wife, it was work, not school. It was not meant to be condescending or anything, but both my Joyces went to school. It just so happened that while one was a student, the other was a teacher. She loved it, being a teacher, but I didn't think I had the patience to do something like that.

The bus came, I got Peanut on it, and I went back inside to find Clara at the table with a bowl of cereal that her mom had given her before she left.

"Good morning, Daddy!" said Clara cheerfully.

"Hi, sweetie, are you ready to have some fun with me before I have to go back to work on Monday?" I asked as I sat down.

"Yep! What are we gonna do today?"

First, we had to go to my mother-in-law's to take care of her coal stove. It was not terribly cold, but she was in her 80s. So keeping her house warm was a priority. I didn't mind doing it; she was family. And she'd watch over Clara instead of us having to put her in a day care or preschool, so that was a bonus.

After that was done, I took Clara to the park and called the hockey guy to get the tickets. While at the park, at the time, I did not take notice, but looking back, maybe it was a sign. A good chunk of the other parents there had hand sanitizers. I knew a stomach bug was going around the school district, but Joyce was not too worried about that because it was mostly in the kindergarten. I guess everyone here had kids in kindergarten.

The day ended with us having our Friday pizza for dinner, which we picked up on our way home from the park. School was done for the week, so both Joyces were happy. I was feeling much better and was ready to go back to the pile of work on Monday. After church on Sunday, we were going to a hockey game. Pretty sweet weekend coming up, eh? How in the hell was I supposed to know it was going to be the last "normal" weekend that we or anyone else in the world were ever going to see again?

March 8, 2020

It was Sunday. I started out this Sunday like I did basically every other Sunday during the school year. I woke up, got the kids ready for Sunday school, and made breakfast. Peanut wanted hard-boiled eggs and toast *and then* only ate the yolk in the middle of the egg and left the white part for me. Clara wanted either waffles or cereal. Today it was cereal. Mom…well, most of the time, Mom got her own breakfast because I rarely made the eggs the way she liked them—fried with the yolks not broken so she could dip her toast in them. It was hard for me to do because I couldn't seem to get the timing down right.

As I got the kids ready to go, I asked Joyce if she wanted to go to church with me. This morning, Joyce took a pass. She was feeling punky, so it was just me and the kids.

The girl's class was small—only five kids including them. The whole Sunday school itself was usually between ten and fifteen kids. The classes used to be bigger up until about two years ago when we lost some members to a new-aged nondenominational church with their big fancy pomp and circumstance and blah, blah, blah. That was not church; that was just a lot of loud noise with the words *Jesus* and *God* sprinkled in there.

It was sort of annoying, the setup, because halfway through the service, I had to leave and get the kids from Sunday school. Just as long as my check cleared, then hallelujah. I got in, said hi to everyone, dropped off my tidings, said a few prayers, and then was out. Generally speaking, there were three things that I prayed for religiously: (1) a healthy family, (2) to hit the lottery (love me my Pick 5 numbers), and (3) some alone time with the wife. I figured if I got one of three, then God was listening, and so far, everyone was pretty healthy. So win-win.

I should have listened harder to the sermon that day. I honestly didn't remember anything about what the pastor said, and seeing now that it would be the last message that he would deliver for a long time, I felt really bad about not listening harder. But I did remember people murmuring about this virus that hit one of the relatives of a member of the congregation over in Italy, Japan, or somewhere. Boy, when I get a chance, I was going to have to search online about whatever the hell this virus was that everyone was talking about, but right now, there was no time for that. It was 11:25 a.m. I had five minutes to get the kids, go home, get the wife, stop and get gas, and then get to the Arena for puck drop.

On the ride over to the arena, Joyce got her bottles of hand sanitizer out and gave one to each of the girls and handed one to me.

"What is this for?" I asked as I struggled to get the damned bottle into my pants while driving.

"Just in case, that is all. Every time someone touches a railing or door handle, make sure you squirt your hands. Everyone got that?" Joyce said in her serious mom/teacher voice.

"Yes, Mom," we all said in unison, basically.

We got to the arena, got our tickets at the will-call office, went through security, and got to our seats about three minutes before the game started. As we got settled in, I went for the usual snack run. No one else wanted to come (or help, ugh), so I got everyone's orders and went on my way. As I made my way for drinks, popcorn, pretzels, and fries, my first thought was, *Wow, the lines are really not that bad.* I knew it was a Sunday afternoon game, which was lightly attended to begin with, but wow, I guessed I got here just in time for everyone to get settled in or whatever. So it was a win for me!

Arms full, I made it back to my seat and started handing everything out. The kids were, of course, gobbling down their stuff as I noticed Joyce started scanning the arena. I started looking around too and saw why the lines were not bad. The place was very lightly attended. I mean, it wasn't a ghost town, but you could definitely tell that there were as not as many people there as there should have been.

"Do you see the same thing that I do?" asked Joyce as she nudged my shoulder.

"Like, how no one is here?" I asked as I continued to scan the arena. "You know, it's a shame. They just resigned this local team to a second ten-year contract, and this is the first season. Everyone in this valley complains that there is nothing to do, but no one comes to the games. Is it that unreasonable for $50 for four people to come out to the games?"

"No, I don't think so, but I just hope it's that. I hope it's not because the team isn't doing that great."

"Meh, I don't know. Given this is the first and only game that we have come out to this year, maybe we don't even have a leg to stand on," I said as I took a drink from my water. Where the heck was everyone?

We were all having a great time at the game. Maybe we were having a little too much fun because a little more than halfway through the game, the group that was in front of us got up. They were a group of four people. It looked like a mom and dad and then their two grown kids. As the dad walked by me, I thought he shot me a look.

Joyce and I looked at each other and shrugged. Yeah, the kids were a little loud, but it was a hockey game, bro. What did you expect? Heck, when they scored a goal, a giant alarm would start blaring. You're telling me the two little kids next to me were that much louder? Give me a break!

The group of four got up and moved down four rows. Aaand they could. The rows in front of them were empty for almost all of the game. No one was coming to claim them, which, okay, was cool. Why were there so many empty seats?

The game ended, and we all got up to leave. I held on to Peanut's hand, and Joyce grabbed Clara's. We all kept an eye on each other as we moved with the group toward the exit. In the parking lot, we made our way out to the car quickly. I got the girls buckled in as Joyce got our stuff into the back of the car. Once we were both done, we got into the front seats.

"Is it me, or is the parking lot, like, empty?" asked Joyce.

"No, it's not just you. It is really empty! Did you notice that group in front of us who moved during the game to new seats?" I asked as I navigated my way out into traffic.

"Oh, those people who moved because the girls were too loud? Yeah, I saw them. I just was surprised as to how much room there was that they could actually move down that far!" said Joyce as she reached back to help one of the kids with something.

"I guess we just picked a good day for a game. Good job, hon," I said.

"Yeah, I guess," said Joyce.

Chapter 2

Day 1

March 9, 2020, Monday

Beep, beep, beep.

I groggily rolled over and slapped my alarm clock off. It was my first day back at work since the surgery. Ugh, I had to get up at four-thirty in the morning again. I sat up and looked over at Joyce. My god, she was beautiful. I leaned over and gave her a really light kiss on her exposed arm and said, "I love you, Joyce. Have a nice day at work."

"Mmm, I love you too," she mumbled as she rolled over to go back to sleep until her alarm goes off in about an hour and a half.

I usually set out my clothes for the next day on the side of the bed so I would not be rummaging around in the middle of the dark at butt-early o'clock and wake everyone up. I grabbed my stuff and headed downstairs to make my coffee then use the bathroom. This had been my routine for years to get ready for work. Work, so where do I work?

I was an inventory control coordinator (ICC) for one of the nation's largest warehousing companies. In a nutshell, our customers were big-name manufacturers that, while they made the product, hired us to store, ship, and tend to whatever they were making. We had accounts all over the world, so if you wanted to transfer somewhere but still stay with the company, it was relatively easy.

The customer I worked with was the nation's leading (and best, in my opinion) juice manufacturer, which was owned by a larger company. They had a warehouse over in Mountain Top, Pennsylvania, which was where I worked—about forty-five minutes away. In 2010, I started out as a yard dispatcher/warehouse coordinator and worked my way over to the inventory spot. I had been there long enough to know that despite all the complaining, all the "tension," and all the normal bullcrap, it was actually a really nice job to have. I had seen so many times people who left within six months came back. Joyce was always telling me, "Just go to work, do your job, and come home to me. We will love you no matter who put the wrong pallet of blue juice next to the pallet of red juice."

Anyway, with my lunch made up, I put it in my lunch box and grabbed my cup of fresh coffee. I didn't buy coffee on the way in because that cost money. No, when Joyce and I were dating, she got me a coffee maker for Christmas that only made three or four cups at a time. It was perfect for me because no one in this house drank coffee. I didn't need a fancy machine or something that made gallons of coffee. This coffee maker was about twelve years old and kept on brewing. She had offered to get me a new one, but why? This thing still worked!

I was out the door at 5:00 a.m. and in my truck. My shift started at 6:00 a.m., but that was because I was there before the rest of the first-shift crew. The building had two inventory people for a place that ran twenty-four hours a day during the week then twelve-hour days on the weekend. So I worked from 6:00 a.m. to 2:00 p.m., and the other inventory guy, Mark, came in for the next shift—2:00 p.m. to 10:00 p.m. That way, there was at least one inventory person on each shift for the week. The weekend, well, I usually just walked into giant pile of "opportunities" on Monday. And given this was a Monday after my vacation, which I took for my surgery, there were many of these "opportunities."

Compounding these issues lately was that we didn't have a first-shift lead/supervisor or a third-shift supervisor. This happened because we had a new building open up, and people were moved around. It was not *impossible* to run the building the way we were currently doing, but when a group of forklift operators didn't have a supervisor to answer too, well, the mice would play, won't they? Because I had been there so long, I had been exposed to almost every problem that you could think of with logistics operations. And I know the system pretty well, so if anyone had problems, I could take care of it. The only thing that I didn't do was handle personnel issues like vacation time, attendance issues, and the forklift computers. That usually fell on my boss, Big Boss.

Big Boss used to be a football player and was pretty much the tallest guy I knew. People would argue with me till the cows came home, but as soon as I said, "Go see Big Boss," yeah, that stopped. This guy was *not* a micromanager. The team he built, myself included, was expected to do what they were supposed to do, and the only reason he would ever get involved would be because it was a fresh, new problem that no one saw *or* something that only he had the authority to do. It was a good and a bad thing. It meant he was mostly agreeable when I came to him with a problem and presented my ideas to fix it. It also meant that the shifts, in some ways, were run differently and that there was a loss of consistency in the operations. While it was negligible, sometimes I got comments like "That is not how we do it on my shift," and I'd usually reply, "That's great. This is how we are going to do it right now." It annoyed me a bit, but it was not like I was stopping the operations. So just deal with it.

I pulled into the parking lot, and it had quite a few cars in it. The building was basically a big box broken up into five sections: the cooler (about one-sixth of the building and where the cold storage was), the front offices (where the administrative staff and bigger bosses worked), the back office (warehouse operations, basically), production (where we mixed juice flavors up on conveyor belts into multipacks), the front docks (dock doors 1–35), and the back dock (doors 42–55). In between all that was five hundred thousand square feet of storage space with racks three levels high. I and three other people had training on equipment to go up into the racks to fix the pallets, and man, did I wish we had another inventory person to help with all of it.

Walking up to the time clock, I passed a few of the yard jockeys talking with the director of transportation. Yard jockeys were the guys who drove the little white trucks that moved trailers around in the yard. The director was the first one to recognize me, smiling and holding out his hand.

"Arty, how you feeling?" he asked.

"A little sore still but okay."

"Are you on any work restrictions?"

He was also the safety director for our building, so I was not surprised that he was asking a question like that.

"No, the doctor only had me off for three days, and if I got any infections or anything like that, I have to give them a call. Otherwise, I won't need a note or anything to come back to work," I replied.

"All right, great! See you around," he said as he walked into the front offices. Only certain employees of my company could go into the front offices. It wasn't always like that until we got new carpeting and one of our jockeys trounced right on it with muddy boots. The front-office people got a little upset at that.

After clocking in, I saw a few of the third-shift forklift operators, and as I looked down at the docks, I couldn't help but notice it was a little busier than I had expected. I mean, it wasn't insane, but there were people from the first shift here on overtime. I looked down the aisles that I knew intimately because when I was not counting their accuracy, I was strapped in a harness, hanging thirty feet in the air, fixing stuff above them. I noticed the aisles weren't all that empty. I knew that we began getting full for the busy season, which was from the end of May to September, but this seemed slightly more than normal.

As I walked down the walkway to the back office, I saw Kurt. Kurt and I had the most time with the company at thirteen years each, but he was at a different building before coming to this one. I flagged him down when he got close enough to see.

"Good morning, Mr. Art!" said Kurt as I shook his hand.

"Hey, Kurt, how are you?" I said as I tried to step out of the way of other forklifts.

"I am okay. How are you? How did the surgery go?" he asked.

"It was fine, thanks. The surgery went okay. Ummm, sooo why is it, like, busier than when I left last week? Are we heavier on the inbounds? It looks a little fuller," I said as I looked around.

"Oooh, yeah, we're getting a little full, but we have a ton of outbounds. The day after you left, the volume picked up," he said.

"Yeah, I can see that. Any problems while I was away?" I asked.

"Of course, but hey, that's job security!" he said with a smile.

We both kind of chuckled at that as I kept on walking toward the back office. The back office had a door to the outside for the truck drivers, four bathrooms, and big open windows so you could see into the warehouse. It was where we held the preshift meetings. It also had the dispatch desk, the inventory desk, the supervisor's desk, and Big Boss's office. I walked in to see the weekend-shift supervisor and the warehouse coordinator (dispatcher, basically), Jim, sitting there in front of a pile of work.

Calieb, the weekend-shift supervisor, was there because the weekend shift was from Friday to Monday. Their operators worked three days, so some took Friday to Sunday while others took Saturday to Monday. Their supervisor, however, had to work from Friday to Monday.

"Hello, Arthur. How did the surgery go?" asked Calieb.

"Yeah, are you now a woman?" asked Jim, who, now with Calieb, was having a healthy laugh.

"Jesus, no, how many times do I have to tell you I did not have gender reassignment surgery?" I said as I walked back to my desk. "What did I miss?"

Calieb came back to my desk to do a quick crossover with me before he left in an hour. "We have a few missing pallets. There are emails out on them. There are two different locations with stuck pallets in them that I did not have a chance to get to."

"I will try to get to the stuck pallets. But I don't want to risk popping a stitch, so we will see. What's with the first-shift operators here so early?" While I was in inventory, I did the preshift meetings until we got a supervisor back, so I did have some awareness of how busy we were.

"Yeah, it's funny. The volume started to pick up a little earlier than normal. We don't see this amount of work for another few weeks, generally. I guess the juice people are getting ready for a busier summer this year. Look at the numbers for today." Calieb handed me the pass-down sheet for the first shift with any special notes for the day like volunteers for overtime and how many trucks we had. I saw the total number of trucks—160. That was about thirty trucks more than I would have expected, especially since there was nothing in the yard.

"A hundred and sixty trucks and none in the yard? Are these all live loads and drops that haven't gotten here yet?" I asked Calieb while reviewing the numbers. Live loads were trucks that needed to be loaded as the drivers arrived while drops were loads that could be dropped in our yard to be loaded or unloaded when we got the chance to do them.

"Yeah, I know. That's a lot of juice," he said.

"Meh, they better sell it before it expires. Otherwise, there are going to be a lot of donations going out, ha!" I said as I got up to go to Big Boss's office. "Big Boss here yet?"

"Hey, Art, how are you feeling?" I heard Big Boss ask from inside his office.

I walked through the door into his office and saw him sitting at his computer. "I am doing okay. Thanks for asking. What did I miss?"

"Juice in and juice out. Before you sit down at your desk, do you want to help me with the KPIs really quick so that I can get these out?" he asked.

"Sure," I said as I took a seat next to him at his desk. At Big Boss's desk, he had a work laptop and a regular computer with two screens so that he could get a lot of work done all at one time. KPIs, or key performance indicators, for our building were a collection of numbers and facts that the company used to judge how well we were performing. The ones that I helped out with—the inventory KPIs—were entered in on a weekly basis. Because I didn't have access to the system, though, I usually helped Big Boss enter them by gathering the information for him and highlighting what he should be entering after he gave them a once-over and either agreed with me or not. Basically, I had to refine readily available information into something for corporate to use to measure how our building was doing against other buildings.

While we were sitting there, reviewing the information for the entries, I couldn't help but notice that one of the two big screens had an email highlighted. I never ever read these out of professional courtesy, but the screen was huge. And it was impossible not to notice an email that was titled "ALL HANDS ON DECK," which was sent by one of the big bosses for the juice people last week. That title, the *title by itself*, gave me pause. The email screen had one column for inbox notifications from who sent the email, the second column was for the email title, and a third column gave you a preview of the email. As we kept scrolling the pages on the screen, I couldn't help but notice the preview of the body of the email:

> Team, you may want to prepare your folks for increased overtime, and to be ready to work mandatory 12s because, as you are all aware, our volume is drastically and quickly increasing because of...

And that was all that the preview showed, but it was enough to get my mind going. Jesus, because of why? Wow, the person who sent this email was higher up on the chain than my boss, so he was seeing something that we were not. Yet nowhere on the shift notes was there a mention of mandatory overtime, increasing the volume, or any kind of warning, though anyone paying attention to the numbers would notice the unexpected increase. I didn't dwell on it too much because there was still a lot on my plate already, and I hadn't even started at my own desk. I finished up helping Big Boss and then went to my workstation.

Under normal circumstances, I'd take a look at any pending emails from the juice people first then work on any problems left over from the previous shift (trucks that were wrong, products that were wrong, products that were broken, products that were missing, etc.). I'd then begin to work on freshness for the day, looking at what products had orders and their current shelf life and trying to make sure that we were getting the oldest stuff out first. At the moment, though, I had to look at any emails about messages for the forklift operators, current freight volumes, and other issues that inventory didn't normally handle because of our staffing levels in the office. I was here to help keep everything moving along regardless of what my actual title or work responsibilities were.

At 7:00 a.m., the first shifted started, and I stepped out of the shipping office onto the warehouse floor where everyone was grouped together. Big Boss wasn't on the floor yet, and because everyone knew that I couldn't access the time clock system on the computer, they didn't ask me about attendance issues, vacation times, etc.

"Good morning, everyone. We have 160 trucks to do today, 50 inbounds, 2 of them live loads, 105 outbounds…105 outbounds?" I asked quizzically as I looked back into the office at Jim. He was the one who prepared the crossover meeting notes. I just looked at the total at the bottom of the sheet. I did not expect so many outbounds because of the fact that it was early March. Who the heck was drinking this much juice in early March? These should be inbounds, preparing us for the busy season. This was way too many outbounds, and at this rate, our building was going to be empty waaay before June.

"It's correct, Artie," said Jim in response to my shock.

"Okay, then, 105 outbounds with 40 of those being live loads and 5 in the yard left for the day." As I read the notes, I noticed that we were asking for the max number of volunteers to come in early before we ran out of forklifts for everyone to use. "We need five people in early tomorrow, two or four hours." Kurt put up his hands first, and then I got four more volunteers out of roughly fifteen forklift operators. I then told everyone that the remainder of the shift was on mandatory ten hours.

"Any questions?" I asked.

"Hey, yeah, are we still calling you Art, or did you pick a new name?" said the one operator I called Wisecracker, to which the entire shift was thunderously laughing. He was a real ball buster. But he knew his stuff, so it was a double-edged sword. He was also the weekend-shift lead at our other building.

"You're a real SOB, you know that? How many times do I have to tell everyone I did not get gender reassignment surgery? Okay, that's it. Everyone, be safe," I said as I went back into the office to grab my work and get on my forklift to start working on the floor.

While I was out on the floor, operators always stopped to ask me questions, and I was normally okay with helping them out. Without a supervisor, I usually could answer most questions on my own from what I have learned over the years. If it was a missing pallet, I'd usually find it. If the pallet was stuck in the racks, I could usually get it down with some extensions we had for our forklifts or a different recovery technique that I had learned. If the pallet was damaged, I'd work with the operators to get it fixed and ship it out. That was pretty much my entire day.

"Art, do you copy?" I heard over the personal radios that we carried.

"Yeah, go ahead."

"Art, it's Kurt. Do you have time to help me get a pallet down? It's in pretty bad shape."

"Yeah, I can give you a hand. Where are you?" I asked as he flagged me down while I drove by him. The pallet had broken though the racks, which did happen occasionally, but the problem was you couldn't get under it. He gave me his lift, and I worked slowly to lift the pallet with his lift so that we could get the pallet positioned where you could place it down on the racks and slide the fork blades under it. You needed to really pay close attention to how the forklift was reacting; you couldn't just jam yourself into it and hope for the best. Make the corrections you need to as you are working it, and the pallet would come out just fine. And with that, I got the forks under the pallet and got it safely onto the ground, where it could be put onto a new one and shipped.

"You're the man, Arty. You're the man!" quipped Kurt as I got down from his lift.

"I try to be as good as you, but I can't, Kurt," I said.

"Oh, listen to you…"

"I hope you do because no one else will!" I joked as I got back into my forklift and carried on with my business.

There were forklifts everywhere, zipping between the trailers and the warehouse. What struck me was that we were moving waaay more product out than we should be at this time. We normally began bulking up for the busy season, so the place was normally wall-to-wall with juice, but not at the moment.

I could be on the floor for hours before I needed to go back into the office, and it was close to 1:00 p.m. when I headed back to my desk.

"Hey, where have you been all day?" asked Big Boss as he walked by my desk.

"Well, good afternoon, sir. You guys left me quite a pile for when I got back. What did you expect!"

"I forgot to ask you this morning. How did the surgery go? How are you feeling?"

"The surgery went okay. I was down for about two days at home, but once I started moving around, it was like nothing ever happened. How was it here without me?" I asked back.

"We managed, but no more surgeries this year, okay?" he laughed as he headed back to his office.

"Yeah, I am not making any promises on that one, boss!" I yelled back.

Last year in September, I left work early for the first time in thirteen years with terrible abdominal pains. Turned out, after being in the ER for twelve hours, that I was having a gallbladder attack and had to get it removed. I was out of work for four weeks then on light duty for an additional three weeks. I had always joked that the only way people would know I was done with that place was when there was a chalk outline of me on the floor. On that particular day, that was not too far from the truth!

"How about it? Okay, I have a conference call to be on, so if I don't see you, have a nice day," said Big Boss as he closed the door.

"Thanks!" I said as I turned back to my computer.

At 1:30 p.m., I began shutting down for the day, putting up my away message, cleaning the workstation and the forklift, and answering any last-minute emails. I was getting it ready for when the second-shift inventory guy, Mark, came in.

Mark had been with us for about three years. He had left last year to go work for a different company but then decided to come back. He did this at the same time that his replacement was getting ready to quit, so it worked out for everyone.

I closed up my workstation and began walking up to the time clock. Now, at this point, the overtime people from the second shift were here (they got here at 1:00 p.m.), so I was being cautious not to get in anyone's way. I knew that I had the right of way while walking down the docks in the crosswalk, but if the operator didn't see me, then the only thing that would be right away would be another trip to the hospital. Mark was waiting at the time clock when I got there.

"Hey, there he is. How are you feeling?" asked Mark as he clocked in.

"I am feeling okay, a little sore after being on the lift all day. I did not expect that. How are you? What did I miss?"

"Well, the usual. Is it getting a little busier than it is supposed to. You have been here longer than me. Am I not the only one seeing this?"

"Yeah, this is a bit unusual." I totally didn't want to let on that I saw an email basically saying that we should all hold on to our butts.

"Okay, well, anything pressing going on?" asked Mark.

This was the inventory crossover at this point where I'd tell Mark what, if anything, was going on with our inventory workload. I gave him the rundown of what was going on—missing pallets, quality holds, or anything else that I didn't get to during my shift, which he would have to hit right out of the gate when he started. After that, at 2:00 p.m., it was quitting time!

I headed out to the parking lot quickly. On the way home, I wanted to stop and get some garlic bread for dinner at the grocery store. Because school didn't get out until 3:30 p.m., the Joyces usually weren't home until 4:00 p.m. And Clara stayed with my mother-in-law, so I had a bit of time to do a little odds-and-ends grocery shopping.

The grocery store was a little busy for a Monday. I literally needed only one thing, so naturally, I got up to the register with ten. I hated when that happened, but I was an impulse buyer. I was such a sucker for any good deals like reduced-price meat or cheese because they were getting old or daily specials that they ran. I didn't spend more than $40 at a time, which was my only restriction. Problem was, sometimes I'd stop almost every day when coming home from work for one thing or another.

I got home about forty minutes before everyone else got home, so I immediately started making dinner. I tried to have dinner ready for when everyone got home so that it would be the first thing we did. I prepped the homemade pasta sauce (I made my own because Joyce had high blood pressure, so if I did it, I didn't add salt; it was still pretty good) and got everything ready to start making the pasta. While I set the water to boil and preheated the oven for the garlic bread, I went outside and got in our "buggy" to go up to Grandma's house to get Clara and work on her coal stove. The buggy was a side-by-side quad that we bought because in the wintertime, my mother-in-law's driveway was so bad that we couldn't get cars up and down it. Without this thing, we would be in some trouble.

I got up to her house. While she was our next-door neighbor, she was near the top of the mountain, so she was a couple of a hundred feet above us. I took care of her coal stove. Meanwhile, Clara was old enough to get herself ready to go home with the putting on of her snow boots and coat and everything. She just needed help with her gloves, which Grandma took care of. By the time I was done with the coal stove, Clara was already waiting for me in the buggy.

When Clara and I got back down to the house, I took care of our coal stove next while she went in and greeted our dogs—Shaggy and Buster. After I finished doing what I was doing and Clara was finished getting undressed, the water for the pasta was boiling, and the oven was ready for the bread. The pasta sauce was also ready to go, and all the while, I still had five minutes before the Joyces got home.

As I started to get the pasta going, my wife, Joyce, walked through the door. I stopped what I was doing, turned around, and went over to give her a kiss.

"Hey, hon. How was your day?" I asked as Clara came running around the corner, screaming, "Mommy!"

"It was fine. How are you feeling? Your thing doing okay?"

"The bouncing around on the forklift made it uncomfortable, but the doc was right. It really is a pretty quick recovery. Do you want to go out and wait for Peanut so I can finish up dinner?" I asked as I put the garlic bread into the oven.

"Sure. Clara, want to come outside and wait too?" asked my wife, Joyce.

"No, it's too cold outside, Mom," said Clara.

Joyce and I laughed as she went to go back outside, but she stopped short as she overheard the TV. In the background, I had the news on the little TV we had in the kitchen to wait for the weather. As it was going through its normal routine of local house fires and car crashes, it began a segment on the COVID-19 virus and what was going on around the world. Major cities were on lockdown, people were not moving, and quarantines of people coming back into the US on planes and boats. It gave Joyce pause as she went back outside. I didn't know how she was going to take me telling her that I saw a confidential email saying that things were going to get super busy.

Little Joyce came home, and we had dinner. After that, while I played with Clara, little Joyce and Mom went over her homework. She had a new list of spelling words that I had to bring up to her bedroom to go over with her. When I put Peanut to bed, we usually went over her spelling words, and then in the morning, Joyce would review a second time with her before she went to school. It was why she had a 100 percent average in spelling, but her actual English grade was around a 75 or 80 percent. It was really funny, how that worked.

The rest of the night was just a normal night at our house. The kids played upstairs, my wife, Joyce, relaxed on her recliner chair, I relaxed on the couch, and the dogs…well…licked themselves, for the most part. We had a two-year-old dachshund named Buster and a fourteen-year-old cocker spaniel named Shaggy (we called him the old man because he was deaf and nearly blind). When the time came, Joyce and I had it set up that I'd put the kids to sleep because she was the one at home that got them ready in the morning and put them on the bus to go to school.

I got the kids upstairs and brushed their teeth and mine, and tonight they wanted to sleep in the same room together. Joyce and I were fine with it because when they slept in separate rooms, sometime in the middle of the night, either one of them would get up and just simply walk into the other's room to go to sleep because they loved being next to each other—well, when they weren't beating each other up over a stupid video game or something,

After getting the girls settled and doing our normal night routine, I kissed them both good night, tucked them into little Joyce's bed, and told them good night. I walked down the hall into my and my wife's room to find her on the bed with coupons.

"You know, hon, if you want me to do something to you, we have to wait because I am still recovering. So just hold on to those coupons, beautiful," I playfully said as I snuggled up next to her and gave her a kiss on the forehead.

"What? No, listen, I need you to do something for me."

She tried to hand me a fistful of coupons to the local hardware store.

"What's this?"

"I want you to stop at the hardware store and, using these coupons, pick up a couple of N95 respirator masks."

"The kind that they use for painting or in those sci-fi movies about virus outbreaks?" I asked.

"Yes, Arthur, I am telling you I have a bad feeling about what is going on. I know you might think I am crazy, but please, can you do this for me? For us?" Joyce at this point was being very serious and concerned as I took the coupons from her.

"Actually, Joyce, I don't think that your crazy because..." This was where I told her about the email I saw. Her face got even more concerned.

"So what is going to happen at work?" she asked.

"I know it's not the summer, when this normally happens, but Joyce, if they are telling my bosses that we need to prepare for mandatory twelve-hour days in March with weekends, I mean, you may not see me for a while."

"What did they tell everyone you work with?" asked Joyce.

"That is the thing. They have not said anything to anyone. I don't know if they are waiting for a special time or something, but if I were them, I would be telling everyone now so that their families have time prepare," I said as I took the coupons and got into bed.

"Do you guys have enough workers?" she asked.

"Oh no, it is still the winter. We just started training forklift operators for the summer months, and they never got anyone to replace the supervisor on our shift. It is basically just me and the dispatcher running the building with Big Boss," I said.

"I hate when you work the weekends," said Joyce.

"That's why I generally don't volunteer," I said as I took her hand. "It wouldn't be so bad to have some extra money for coal and stuff, though."

As Joyce cleaned up the coupons and got into bed, she said, "Well, if they need you at work, then I guess they need you at work, but please do not forget that you have a family that needs you too."

Chapter 3

Day 2

March 10, 2020, Tuesday

Beep, beep, beep.

I groggily rolled over and slapped my alarm clock off. It was my second day back at work, and all the bouncing around on the forklift had kind of irritated my unmentionables. I sat up and looked over at Joyce. My god, she was beautiful. I leaned over and gave her a really light kiss on her exposed—blasted, what the heck was she lying like this for?—her exposed shoulder blade. "I love you, Joyce. Have a nice day at work."

Driving in to work, I'd usually listen to the radio. I listened to talk radio because of the politics and news. But this morning, instead of the normal blah-blah-blah, yadda-yadda-yadda politics, the tone was more rushed and worried. They were talking about this new virus, the efforts overseas to stop it, the days of people being quarantined on the ships, the first outbreak in the US at a nursing home in Kirkland, Washington, etc. Whatever, I was just waiting for the weather to come on really quick before I pulled into the employee parking lot.

As I start walking to the entrance of the building where the time clock was, I was struck by the amount of live tractor trailers waiting in the yard. Normally, at this time of year, there would maybe be one or two. But I counted eight, not including the yard trucks that were used for the preloaded outbounds. It was a flurry of activity. But again, it was the beginning of March…so what the heck was going on?

I clocked in and headed toward my cubicle, which was in the shipping office—about the midway point of the building. As all the forklifts buzzed around with the backup sirens and the horns blowing, I looked at the volume of the warehouse itself. I could tell just from eyeballing it that we should be around 80 percent full but were hovering somewhere around 55 percent or 60 percent at the moment. Not only did I know this because I was "inventory Jesus," but from just looking around, you'd notice that the entirety of the top racks, which should be full, were all empty.

"Hey, Art. Good morning. Listen, I hate to hit you with these, but…" Jim started talking as I entered the office. Because they didn't have an inventory person or a supervisor, it was tough on him, so I just took whatever issues he had off his hands and tried to fix them. It was nothing super critical, but as he handed me some papers for trucks that had the wrong product or for problems with the order allocation, he also handed me the pass-down for my shift. We had 180 outbound trucks. This was not the total amount of trucks, which was, well, past 200 trucks, but 180 outbounds.

"Whoa, you feeling okay this morning, Jim, or did you not do your math right?" I asked as I pointed to the paperwork he handed me.

"No, it's right. I can't believe it either. This is nuts. We're probably going to be mandated this Saturday," he said with a sigh.

"That will be the day, Jim. There is no way they are going to mandate in March. They probably won't want to pay me the overtime," I said as I logged in to my computer. When it finally did fire up and after I opened up my reports, I went to a report that inventory has access to but other positions don't to see if Jim was right. And sure enough, he wasn't wrong.

Looking at the outbound volumes, I did see one interesting thing, which was that it wasn't necessarily the juice that was leaving very quickly. Oh, sure, that was a part of all the volume, but what was really leaving was the water—just plain-Jane, run-of-the-mill water and juice. All I could think at the time was, *Huh?*

I finished fixing the problems Jim gave me and then jumped into the inventory emails. Nothing was too spectacularly wrong, so after I was done, I started to look to see if there was anywhere I could help out with the trucks. Right before the first shift started, Big Boss came through the door.

"Good morning, boss," I said as I stood up.

"Good morning, guys. Jim, how are we looking?" asked Big Boss as he walked by Jim and me.

Jim started going over the numbers to the wide-eyed boss.

"Hey, boss, there are no pressing inventory issues that I need to tackle. Do you want me to hop on the trucks?" I asked.

"Yes, please, if you can. We're going to need the help. Tell everyone about mandated ten-hour days and to begin signing up for the weekend," replied Big Boss.

"Not a problem. But the weekend, you sure you want me to announce that?" I asked as I headed out the door to start the shift. He looked at me and nodded his head. "You got it."

When the shift got mandated overtime, generally, the inventory team was exempt because of equipment availability issues, but sometimes I felt a little animosity or resentment that I got to go home on time. But that all would fade when I lumped pallets all by myself and no one gave me any help.

I did the preshift meeting and let everyone know what was going on. There were no real questions but a lot of quizzical looks—very similar to the ones that I personally had when the information was first given to me. I tried to make everyone feel slightly better about the situation.

"Yeah, I know. I am with you guys. This is definitely weird. But there is nothing that we cannot accomplish here, so just get it done!" I said, trying to rally everyone. It did not work well, but I didn't really stick around for people to dwell on it. I grabbed the paperwork for my first truck and went to work.

The rest of the day was just me dealing with the normal issues, only I had to work on them slightly faster. I had volunteered to do trucks, so now I had to work on my truck *and* work on the missing pallets, broken pallets, wrong pallets, long pallets, tall pallets, short pallets, and everything in between. The one good thing about it being so busy was at least the day went by quicker.

I was so busy that I really didn't pay much attention to the clock on the wall of the office as I came to hand in some paperwork. But I did look up, and after running around all morning, I was a little shocked to see that it was almost one-thirty in the afternoon already. I started my normal routine of shutting down my desk and trying to remember anything that happened during the day for my crossover with Mark. I signed off my computer and headed up to the time clock, where I found him getting there to clock in for his shift.

"Hey, buddy," said Mark as I was getting closer to greet him. "Anything going on?"

"Not really, just same old stuff but a lot more of it for some reason," I replied as I went to punch out. "Wife has me doing the weirdest errands today too."

"Oh yeah, what's that? You getting lucky?" he asked excitedly.

"Ha ha, no, I have kids. Anyway, she gave me coupons for the hardware store and asked me to stop there on my way home from work," I said.

"What? Why?" he asked.

"She wants me to pick up gas masks," I said.

"You mean, like, respirators? For, like, when you're doing drywall or painting?" he asked while standing there, looking at me, confused.

"Yeah, something like that. She said as long as it's N95 rated," I said.

"What does that mean?" asked Mark as he started walking toward the shipping office.

"I don't know. Probably means I am going to have to spend more money," I said as we both laughed pretty good at that one.

I told Mark to have a nice day and that I would see him tomorrow. I clocked out then headed to my truck so that I could go to the hardware store. I loved that store. They had tools and little knick-knacks for around the home and my shop (which is basically the part of the house none of the girls wanted because it got super cold in the winter, so I put all my tools in it). The stuff there was of decent quality and cheap. I never needed to get a gas mask there before, though. This should be interesting.

I walked into the store, and the one thing that I just couldn't stand about this place was that there were never enough people to help. Often, it was just one register open and maybe a stock person. I don't know. I eventually did track down someone and asked them where the gas masks were.

"Umm, if we have any left, they will be against the back wall in the middle, next to the painter's tarps," replied the kid. When I asked him if they had any N95 or better masks, he responded with, "Also, sir, what we have out is what we have in inventory. We don't have any in the back, and no, we do not know when we are getting our next delivery."

What the heck did he mean when he said "If there are any left" and "No, we don't have any in the back"? When I got to where he was talking about, I was shocked. I snapped a picture of what I saw and sent it to Joyce.

The wall was empty. Except for two masks, their entire inventory of different sizes and types were gone. The two that were left were for adults, and they were massive—I mean, like, straight up right from an NBC (nuclear, biological, and chemical) suit from the military. There were no replacement filters either. Those were all gone too. What the heck was going on? Was there a big run on drywall and painting jobs?

I quickly grabbed the two masks and headed straight for the register. I didn't even have time to do my normal "Oh, I wish I had this" looking around at the power tools. I did have time to send Joyce a panicked message on social media.

I got up to the register and paid for my stuff just in time to hear the next customers walking through the door and asking the cashier where the gas mask things were. Back at my truck, I called Joyce.

"Hey, okay, so did you see the message I just sent you?" I asked Joyce as I buckled my seatbelt.

"You're kidding me! Yes, I saw it. Oh man, did you get those masks at least?" she asked with a hint of a worried tone in her voice.

"Yes, I did. They were completely out of filters too. I cannot believe that. They said they don't know when they are going to get more in." I started my truck and began to drive home.

"Okay, just come home. I want to tell you what happened at school. I love you."

"I love you too, hon. Bye," I said. I then hung up and headed home.

As I pulled into the driveway, Joyce was standing in the yard, waiting for me. She was home before I was today because I had to stop and spend all that time at the store. I grabbed my lunch box and coffee cup and began walking up to her. Without asking, she took my coffee cup and lunch box away from me when I got to her, gave me a quick kiss, and said, "I need you to go right now to the hardware store in West Pittston by the football field."

I pausing for a second at what she just said. "Oooh-kaaay, any particular reason why?"

"I called down there. They have masks left. You need to go right now and buy them."

"Okay, but can I at least—"

She cut me off.

"You need to go right now, Arthur. I will get dinner and the kids. Please go get them." She had this weird, stern, super serious look on her face.

"Oh… Oh, okay. I love you," I said as I climbed back into my truck.

"I love you too," she said, and she went to go back into the house.

Oh, come on, Joyce. I was just downtown. Why am I going back down again? I thought. *No, no, Arty. Don't say that. Just head back downtown, go to the hardware store, and get the rest of what she needs.* This hardware store was about twenty minutes away, so I knew I was going to be out for at least another hour or so for the round trip.

Now it was getting to be evening when I pulled into the parking lot of the second store. This hardware store wasn't a national name. It was a local mom-and-pop one. The owners were very nice people, but generally, because it was not on my way home, I did not stop here. I walked into the store and asked where the masks were.

"Oooh, are you the husband of the wife that just called a while ago?" asked the girl at the register.

"Yeah, that's me. Do you happen to have any left?" I asked.

She pointed to where the paint supply was. Again, my jaw hit the floor—just two left. There were literally a dozen spots for these things on the wall, but just two left? One was very cheaply made, and the other was a little on the pricier side. I reasoned that because of that, the two together equaled a decent price, so I picked them up. One would definitely fit on the kids, but the other one was, eeehhhh, maybe. I picked them both up as someone was walking in, asking the girl at the register if they had any respirators left.

"No, ma'am, I'm sorry. I just happened to get the last one on the shelves," I said sheepishly as I paid for them.

"Miss, we also do not have any coming in anytime soon. They are all on back order," said the cashier as they handed me my change and receipt. The person who came in promptly followed me out of the store as I left, continuing to talk.

"Oh, it's okay. My husband sent me in here looking for them. I will just tell him they are out," said this nice older lady who apparently had no problem with me having them and was just in there because someone told her to go in.

"Oh, really? That's funny because my wife sent me here too. What the heck is going on with everyone?" I asked as I was walking next to her while going out of the door of the store.

"Oh, who knows? When you have been married for as long as I have, you learn not to argue and that it's just easier to do what they ask," she said as she got back into her car, which was parked next to me.

"Amen to that!" I said as we both got into our cars, and I headed home.

When I got home, Joyce had gotten Peanut off the bus and Clara down from Grandma's. As she finished up dinner, I got our coal stove taken care of and then hopped in the buggy to head up to Grandma's to take care of hers. She was downstairs when I got there, and she asked how my day was. I told her about how crazy it was, how all the gas masks were sold out, and that Joyce had me on a wild-goose chase around the valley for these things. I was not much in the mood for conversation at this point because I wanted to get some dinner, so I quickly headed back home. When I walked through the door and took off my boots, it was just my wife, Joyce, at the dinner table.

"What happened to the kids?" I asked as I sat down for dinner.

"They ate a while ago. It is just me waiting for you," said Joyce as she looked over at the gas masks I had gotten. "This pretty blue one is much smaller, so I think I will use this one if I have to. Or should I save it for the kids? I don't know."

"The two I got from the first hardware store are for adults. I am going to start carrying one with me in case I am somewhere and don't feel comfortable," I said as I took one of the bigger ones and examined it. It was large and cumbersome, and it probably wasn't really designed to be comfortable. Effective, yes, but definitely not comfortable.

"Good idea. We have four total, so I will use the other bigger one. And we can save the small ones for the girls if we need it," said Joyce as we both put them down together.

"What the heck is going on? Did you see the pictures I sent you?"

"Artie, I am telling you I don't have a really good feeling about this. This is bigger than the flu and waaay bigger than H1N1. Something about this one feels different. At least we got the masks before it got to the point where we cannot find them anywhere," said Joyce.

"Hon, you are telling me people were still trying to find masks as I came out of the store with the last two! Is anyone talking about it at the school?" I asked.

"There are rumors that they might be shutting the schools down, but that is all talk right now. A lot more people have been needing my hand sanitizer, so I think I am going to go to the grocery store tomorrow and pick up some more," said a worried Joyce.

"Good move," I said. "If anything really gets shut down, I will fill all the gas cans we have. Also, how about tomorrow I stop at the school to pick up Peanut on the way home and get a load of coal? I will check the temperature in the morning and make the call. The coal breaker is right across the bridge from the school. While we are doing that, you can come home, get Clara, and go to the grocery store."

"Okay, yeah, that will work," said Joyce as she turned on the news. Italy had expanded its quarantine to the entire nation. The entire country of Italy—a country of more than sixty million people—had told its population that they must essentially shelter in place as a last means of defense to avoid a shutdown of the medical system. Joyce and I just looked at each other in shock as the news broadcast went on to explain that, while up until this point, only certain cities were on lockdown. The entire country now had been quarantined. The virus was hitting their substantial elderly population quite hard as the country struggled to keep everything together.

"What?" was what Joyce was able to gasp out.

"Joyce, I am sure that the government is working hard to keep it out of the United States." I tried in vain to reassure her. Unfortunately, I was very, very wrong. At home, forty United States universities and colleges have suspended classes, and New York had surpassed Washington as the state with the largest amount of coronavirus cases. Large United States cities like NYC, Philly, and Baltimore were trying to brace for what could be a very bad situation if it was allowed to get out of control.

"How is it at work?" Joyce asked as the local sports coverage on the news began in the background.

"Joyce, it's nuts. I might have to start staying for overtime if it gets any busier."

"In March? In winter? Do you think that they really are going to ask you to stay for overtime?"

"If they do, do you want me to stay?"

More often than not, Joyce would rather see me home with the kids than be at work. With our combined salaries, it is not entirely necessary that I get a lot of overtime, which is nice. If I had a big bill coming up, I'd usually ask Joyce if I could stay for overtime, and if it was a legitimate concern, she normally wouldn't have a problem with it.

"Yeah, better try to start saving up money just in case," said Joyce with a sigh.

Joyce and I finished up dinner and put everything away. I began to review spelling words with Peanut as Clara played with Buster and Shaggy. It was much too cold to go outside, and it was already dark at this point. Everyone gathered in the living room when we were all done playing with the dogs or doing work. We watched some cartoons on TV until it was time to go to bed.

With the teeth brushing done, the girls and I piled into Peanut's bed. We reviewed her spelling words, and she spelled them with ease. With everything now done for the night, I gave each of them a quick kiss on the head.

"Good night, Joyce, Clara. Daddy loves you."

"Good night, Dad," said little Joyce first.

"Yeah, good night, Dad. I love you too," said Clara.

"You girls both be good for Mom tomorrow, okay? Clara, be good for Grandma too."

"We will, Dad," they both said as I closed the door.

While I was putting the kids to bed, wife Joyce locked up downstairs. The dogs went out in the heated mudroom for the night, and she turned off all the lights. She came to the top of the stairs just as I was closing the kids' door behind me.

"Want to cuddle for a little bit?" I ask sheepishly, not knowing exactly how Joyce was feeling.

"Sure, just let me brush my teeth first."

As I got into bed and waited, I turned on the TV to something other than a news channel, leaned over, and set my alarm clock for the next day. Lord knows we didn't need to see any more news at the moment. I could hear Joyce finish up in the bathroom, and then I heard her footsteps.

She opened the door, and there she was. While she thought nothing of how she looked, I always thought she looked amazing.

"Joyce, have I had a chance to tell you today that I think you are the most beautiful woman in the world and that I am so happy that I married you?"

She climbed into bed then into my arms, saying softly, "I love you too."

As we watched TV, I could tell something was bothering her as she lay with her head on my chest, above my heart.

"You okay, hon?" I asked as I brushed her hair.

"Art, what happens if what is going on over in Italy and everywhere else happens here? Do you think we will be okay?"

I gave her a kiss on the top of the head. "As long as you, the kids, your mom, and I are safe, we will be okay. You and I will both do everything we can to keep everyone safe."

I would stroke her hair until either her or I fell asleep. In this particular case, I didn't know who was first. Usually, I was the one who'd fall asleep first, not her. But it didn't matter at the time because we were all together and safe…for now.

Chapter 4

Day 3

March 11, 2020, Wednesday

Beep, beep, beep.

I groggily rolled over and slapped my alarm clock off. It was my third day back at work, and man, did my crotch ache. *What the heck, man?* I sat up and looked over at Joyce. She was more beautiful than yesterday. I leaned over and gave her a really light kiss on her exposed—*How are you lying now? Ugh*—nape of her neck. "I love you, Joyce. Have a nice day at work." She was still sleeping. Sometimes I wondered if she knew that I did this.

I did my normal routine: say hi to the dogs, make coffee, get lunch ready, make sure the dogs have water in their water bowl, etc. As I grabbed my keys, which hung right next to our digital meteorological station, I saw that it was thirty-one degrees outside—just below freezing.

"Hmmm, how much do you want to bet, Art, that we need coal?" I muttered to myself. See, we had a coal bin that I built that held one and a half tons—give or take—of coal. For my mother-in-law, I built a one-ton coal bin right next to her house and a seven-ton coal bin on one side of her property because of how sometimes in the winter, we could not get vehicles up and down her driveway. I filled her coal bin around September, and ours, I got as we needed. Doing this for so long, I knew that when our coal bin was around half full, we had two weeks left to burn, give or take.

I turned on the TV to watch the local weather, and for the whole week, the temperature at night was going to hover around freezing. Joyce wouldn't let me turn off the coal stove until it was at least fifty degrees outside, so I got out a pen and paper and left a note for Joyce:

> Hey, beautiful, we need to get another load
> of coal. I will get Peanut from school. Text me.
> Love you.

I left the note on her side of the table and headed off. Boy, it was chilly outside. The ride in was not too eventful. Maybe slightly heavier truck traffic, but meh, nothing terrible. That changed when I got into the parking lot. Not only were there trucks everywhere; they must have asked people if they wanted more overtime because the employee parking lot was packed.

I was walking up the sidewalk to the employee entrance when a group of yard jockeys passed me.

"Good morning, team," I said to them with a smile.

"Yeaaah, you won't say good morning when you get in there," replied one of them.

"Why? What now?" I asked.

"We just got told we are going to be mandated overtime this Saturday. They told the third shift tonight," was the reply.

As I was walking up to the door, there were some third-shift employees on a smoke break already complaining about having to work on Saturday. They were mostly upset that they were already mandated overtime and hated to have to work more. I couldn't say that I blamed them. We had to explain to our families now why we were mandated overtime in the winter. What was going to happen when it starts getting warm!

I sat down at my desk, and Jim plopped the pass-down on my keyboard. "Well, there you go. Hope you had better luck than I did with this."

"Oh, calm down, Jim, what is so... Is this right?" I asked with a raised voice.

Jim nodded his head as the first thing I saw was the number of total trucks for the day. There were 224 trucks. Now I saw why they were mandating Saturday; we were not going to be able to catch up even with every forklift we have going. Work was already backed up. I wouldn't be surprised if they mandated Sunday, but I wouldn't tell Joyce that. She didn't really like it when I got overtime because we valued time with the kids more.

I finish what work I could before the preshift meeting while trying to help Jim and the third-shift operators get through their day. A pallet wouldn't scan to the truck. There was product damage. "What do we do?" Products were in the wrong place, there were pallets stuck, and on and on. Boy, did I wish they had an inventory person on the third shift. I put the pass-down on Big Boss's desk so he could write down how much overtime there was, any special projects he had for anyone, and anything else he wanted to pass along to the shift.

Big Boss came walking through the door right before the preshift meeting; said good morning to Jim, me, and a few of the operators; and went into his office.

"*What! Is this right?*" we all heard him scream from his office.

We all kind of froze, and then Jim and I looked at each other and went into the office. Big Boss looked right up at Jim.

"Tell me this is a joke," said Big Boss.

"No, it's not a joke. I already told my guys about Saturday," said Jim.

"Yea? Good. Art, tell everyone that Saturday is going to be a normal scheduled work day. Anyone who doesn't come in is getting an attendance point," said Big Boss.

An attendance point was what you got if you called off work, and a vacation day or voluntary time-off request was not approved. Nine points was how many you could get before you got fired; you'd get fired on your tenth point.

"Got it. Anything else?" I asked.

"No," said Big Boss, and out of the office I went.

I started my preshift meeting right off with the good news, and of course, the groans came. Everyone was now trying to question me.

I told them to go right to Big Boss. How many times did I have to remind people that I was not a supervisor? I didn't have access to the time-clock system. I couldn't enter them in for vacation days. While I could basically do everything else, handling HR-related stuff was the only thing that I couldn't do.

After so many complaints, I just couldn't take it anymore.

"Okay, that's it. Everyone, stop. I keep telling you that complaining to me about the overtime is like complaining to the mailman about your taxes. They are not going to be able to do anything about them, and you still have to pay them," I barked.

That actually did bring out a few chuckles, so now I could get into the meat and potatoes of the preshift meeting. That was when the complaints stopped, and the realization of what was happening hit everyone.

"Art, I am not one to complain," said Kurt, which actually was the case; he very *rarely* complained about anything. "But does anyone know why we are so busy?"

And all I could think about was that email that I had seen two days ago. Someone somewhere knew why we were so busy and was communicating it to our bosses, but for whatever reason, our bosses didn't want to say anything to us.

"I am guessing not because they would probably have told us by now, Kurt. But I am sure there is a reason why everyone is gobbling up this juice like there is no tomorrow," was what I replied. I knew it was a lie, but how exactly was I supposed to tell the truth?

The rest of the day went by with everyone extremely busy, but through all the hustle and bustle, I heard the familiar *ping* and received a text message. It's wife Joyce.

"Got your note this morning. You are to pick up Peanut on your way home after getting coal from school. I am to get Clara and go grocery shopping. Love you."

Even though Joyce and Peanut got out of school at the same time, wife Joyce traveled around between schools. When that happened, she'd beat the bus home, but if she was going to her mom's to get Clara and then go grocery shopping, there might not be anyone home to get Peanut off the bus.

I replied to her text, "Got it. I will pick up Peanut up after getting coal. Have fun. Love you too."

God, did I love her. Every time I got a text from Joyce, it helped me make it through the day. After putting down my phone, I went back to work, trying to organize as much of the craziness as I could.

After work, I headed toward the coal breaker. On the other side of the river in Laflin was where we got our coal. They used to get coal directly across the street from a quarry, but for some reason that they never explained to me, they brought it in by railcar now. The coal was unloaded into a big pile of giant pieces. They scooped them up into conveyor belts that led into a big metal-sided building that, when the crusher was turned on, violently shook as it broke up and spat out different-sized pieces of coal. I had gotten to know the scale master and the heavy-equipment operator pretty well from coming here every year for the past so many years.

I pulled onto the scale so that they could weigh my empty truck empty. The scale master nodded at me and hit the buzzer, and I pulled off the scale and parked under a giant metal hopper at the other end of the yard. In my mirror, I could see the front-end loader behind me, following. I parked under the hopper and got out.

"Hey, bud. How are you?" I asked as I shut my door, and the front-end loader pulled up beside me.

"I'm doing good, bud. What do you need?" he asked from the seat with the door to the machine open.

"I am getting a load for myself, so how about a three-quarter ton of rice?"

Rice coal was a small-sized piece of coal that was used for the automatic-feeding coal furnace that we had. It needed to be small so that it would not jam up the equipment. I let the loader know each time I got a load if I was getting it for myself or my mother-in-law. If it was for me, he knew that he could go a little heavy with the load because the coal bin was in my lawn. If it was for my mother-in-law, he knew that I had to go up the side of a mountain, so he would keep it lighter to avoid too much strain on my truck. Because of where our coal bins were located, they could not just deliver it in a delivery truck, which meant that each time someone needed coal, I had to get it in my truck and shovel it.

"Sure thing, boss," he said as he drove away. A few minutes later, he came from the other side of the breaker with a scoop of that sweet, sweet rice coal. He lifted up the bucket and poured the scoop into the hopper, which funneled it into my truck. After he was done, I waved to him goodbye, drove over to the scale, and got weighed. With the weight of my truck full, they subtracted the weight of my truck empty, and the difference was what I got charged. My truck full is 6,000 pounds. My truck empty was 4,500 pounds. So that meant that I had 1,500 pounds of glimmering coal in the back of my truck, and that was what they charged me for.

After I got the coal, I headed over to the elementary school to get Peanut. She was in the third grade, and she really did love school. She loved her friends, she loved learning, and she loved talking…to everyone…at great length…which could be a problem because she didn't stop talking. Or at least that was what her teacher evaluations said. She was smart, but she talked too much to her friends, drew in class too much, or liked to play too much with her pencils and erasers. The problem was she was pulling 100s in almost every subject. Each night, we went over her spelling work and anything else she had problems with, and while it might seem like she wasn't paying attention, she heard and remembered exactly everything that was said to her. At the parent-teacher conferences, as long as she was not disrespectful, aggressive, or bullying the other kids, Joyce and I both felt that she was fine even though yes, sometimes she did talk too much. I couldn't imagine where she picked that up from.

After picking up Peanut from school, we both headed toward home. I got home and backed the truck up to the coal bin, and we both go to get out.

"All right, hon. Can you do Dad a big favor and start doing your homework while I shovel coal? Either your mom or I will go over it with you when you are done," I asked her as she grabbed her cute little book bag and jumped out of the truck.

"Okay, Dad. Are you going to make dinner?" asked Peanut.

"Uh, yes, after I am done shoveling the coal. Are you hungry now?" I asked, slightly irritated.

"Yeah," she said.

"There are apples in the fridge or pretzels," I told her.

"Ummm, no, can I have ice cream?" she asked with an innocent look on her face.

"Not until after dinner. How about you have a hard-boiled egg? They are in a plastic bag in the fridge," I told her because I knew she liked hard-boiled eggs.

"*Oh boy, okay!*" she shouted and rans into the house after I unlocked the front door for her.

The kid sure did go nuts for hard-boiled eggs, but she was weird because she would tear off all the whites to eat just the yolks. Then she'd leave the pile of eggs on the plate for me. I used them to make a sort of egg-white-salad sandwich with it. Then it was basically the egg whites with mustard.

As I finished up shoveling the coal into the coal bin, wife Joyce pulled into the driveway with Clara and the groceries. As I looked at the car, which was going to park under the carport, I couldn't help but wonder why I could not see over the rear seats. How much food did she buy!

I headed over to the car and opened up the door to Clara's seat to help her unbuckle.

"*Hi, Daddy!*" shrieked Clara as I opened her door.

"Hi, princess. Were you good for Mommy?" I asked.

"She was fine. She was a very good girl," said Joyce as she got out of the car.

I got Clara out, and she ran back into the house as I met wife Joyce and gave her a kiss.

"How was work?" I asked as I went to open the back of her car.

"It was good, but be careful opening that in case something falls out."

I slowly lifted the back of the car and was met by a wall of stuff. Not all of it was food, but there was a lot of that too. She had several packages of toilet paper, paper towels, hand sanitizer, Lysol, and rubbing alcohol as well. She saw the look on my face.

"Art, before you ask, it was nuts down there. People had grocery carts filled to the top. Even Winston and his wife were there," she said.

Winston was someone that my wife's mom worked for as a seamstress. They were better off financially anyway, nice guy. Still, he and his wife were more of special shop patrons than they would be at the local grocery store, so it would definitely be different to see him there.

"Why on earth was Winston there?" I asked as I started pulling the groceries out.

"He and his wife were there buying hand sanitizer," said Joyce.

"Hand sanitizer? Why?" I asked.

"Art, at school today, I had kids coming up to me asking if they could fill their hand sanitizer bottles with my stash because they were out of it at home. So I let them, and now I am completely out. That is why I bought so much today," said Joyce.

"Wait, the kids are out of hand sanitizers at their homes?" I asked.

Joyce handed me some groceries. "It's not just me. All my teacher friends are saying the same thing. People are having trouble getting this hand sanitizer stuff."

"Wow, that is weird. I see you got a lot of canned goods as well as all these paper towels. I mean, wow, Joyce, kind of went overboard with the grocery shopping this week."

"Art, I have a bad feeling about this," said Joyce as we started walking back to the house. "When we left the store, more and more people were coming in. I looked at Clara and said, 'Ready to go back to our home on the mountain, far away from this craziness?' I don't know if I want to go grocery shopping there if it's going to be like that again next week."

"Do you need me to stop on my way home for anything during the week?" I asked.

"No," said Joyce, "but it was just so crazy in there. Sooo many people were buying almost everything. The shelves were starting to go a little bit bare. I don't know when I want to go back, so I over-bought a few things."

"Nothing wrong with that, hon," I said as I started to get stuff into the house.

"Oh, good. Did you get coal?" asked Joyce.

"Yeah, I just finished putting it away. Did you take care of your mom's coal fire?" I asked as I propped open the doors to the house.

"No, can you go do it?" said Joyce.

"After we get the groceries in," I said.

"Okay, if you want to finish this up, I will start dinner. Did Joyce eat anything yet?" asked my wife.

"She said she was going to eat a hard-boiled egg or two." And as I said that, we walked into the kitchen to find two eggs with the yolks ripped out of them. Yeah, she had an egg or two.

I finished getting stuff out of the car and putting them away. I then worked on our coal fire, and when I was done with that, I got into the buggy and went up to Momma Joyce's house. When I went to work on her fire, she was downstairs, working on something on the sewing machine.

"Hey, there you are. How was work?" asked Momma Joyce. She said this as she slowly started to make her way over to me.

Momma Joyce was seventy-nine years young and still kicking. But she was on oxygen, so this little clear cord traveled everywhere she went. One time, she got it wrapped around her coal stove, and it melted to the machine and was feeding the fire pure oxygen. It was pretty warm in the house that day.

"It was okay. Joyce just got back from grocery shopping and said it was nuts. It took me half an hour to empty the car of everything she bought," I replied.

"Weeellll, this virus or whatever is starting to have people scared. I don't know if I want to go to any of my doctor visits," she said to me as I worked on her coal fire.

"Oh no, do you have any coming up soon?"

Momma Joyce had a long, proud history of telling us that she needed to go to the doctors or had any kind of other obligations generally the day before her appointment, giving us little to no time to make arrangements—which was always fun.

"No, not for another month. Can you take those days off to take me to the doctor?" she asked.

"I have some vacation time I can use, yeah. Do you have them on the calendar upstairs?" I asked.

"Joyce knows when they are. You can ask her," she said.

"Okay," I said as I finished up putting coal in her stove and emptying out the ashpan. "Have a goodie."

"Have a goodie" was something my father-in-law used to say to me all the time before he passed away five years ago. I liked it, so I started saying it all the time to my mother-in-law and sometimes to my wife.

"Okay, you too," she replied.

I got back home just in time for everyone to sit down at the table for dinner. After the kids were done eating, they left the table, and wife Joyce and I got some time to talk.

"How was work for you?" asked Joyce as we continued eating.

"I hate to tell you this, hon, but I am mandated to work on Saturday from 6:00 a.m. to 2:00 p.m."

"Oh, come on, seriously? It's the winter. Who is buying juice when it is below thirty-two degrees outside?"

Yeah, I could tell she was upset.

"I know, but we also have water and other stuff that is flying out. There is a weird part to all of it, though," I said as I finished my last bit of food. "We have a lot of stuff going out of the building but honestly, not that much coming into the building. We were full before, so for right now, it's not a bad thing."

Joyce looked over at me and was like, "And so what does that mean?"

"Well eventually, we are going to run out of stuff to ship out, which normally doesn't happen until about late June or the middle of July. It's going to mess up our supply chain at some point because we're going to run out of juice."

"Well, good," said Joyce, smiling at me. "Then maybe you won't get mandated to work on the weekends!"

"Ha," I laughed pretty well at that one. "Yeah, maybe. Hey, before I left your mom's house, she said she has doctor's appointments coming up next month in April and that you knew what the days were. Can you tell me so I can take them off from work? I will take your mom because I know you use up your sick days faster than me."

"Huh? My mom never said anything to me about doctor's appointments," said Joyce.

"Aaand of course she didn't. Ugghhh, fine, I will go back up to her house and look at the calendar," I said.

"Okay, thanks, honey. I love you!" Joyce said to me cheerfully and lovingly (to try to make me feel better about having to go back up there, but she doesn't have to worry because it does make me feel better).

I put my plate in the dishwasher and headed back out to get the dates. I wished I sometimes listened to my instincts as well as Joyce listens to hers. Joyce would have checked *before* she left her mom's house. Oh well, tomorrow was another day.

<h1 style="text-align:center">Chapter 5</h1>

<h1 style="text-align:center">Day 4</h1>

March 12, 2020, Thursday

Beep, beep, beep.

I groggily rolled over and slapped my alarm clock off. It was my fourth day back at work, and man, did my crotch ache worse. I sat up and looked over at Joyce. My god, she was more beautiful than yesterday. I leaned over and gave her a really light kiss on her exposed—oh, for Pete's sake, how was she lying now? I gave her a kiss on her exposed hand. "I love you, Joyce. Have a nice day at work."

It was the same drive into work, and more chatter was on the radio about this stupid cold going around. If it was really that serious, wouldn't you think that the government would have said something already like, "Hey, listen, there is a stronger-than-normal flu season this year, so just be on your toes a little"? There was not a peep from anyone, so this is all probably just media hype. It was getting so annoying that I turned off my normal talk radio and put on the country music station just to get something out of that machine that was a little more positive.

I pulled into the parking lot, and once again, more trucks were waiting than there should've been this time of year. It was cold as get out. What the heck were people doing, drinking all this juice? I guessed you still had to stay hydrated, but damn.

The day was very busy, but it was Thursday. So the madness wouldn't end when I clocked out. It was also dance day, so now that I had pretty much recovered from the surgery, it was my job to take the girls to their dance class. Each year, when we signed the kids for dance at the end of September, they had three choices: hip-hop, tap, and ballet. Joyce was in tap right now, and she was doing fantastic. Clara was in ballet, and she loved it, not to mention looked *adorable* doing it. If we had the money for it, they could do all three of the styles, but that was a lot of money and time, quite frankly. Some parents did it and treated it like day care, where they dropped off the kids at whatever time and, in an hour and a half later, picked them up. I wouldn't be opposed to it, but jeepers, that was a lot of money. Nah, onc class, and wc wcrc good.

Once I finally did clock out, it was like the race was on. I had to fight the traffic outside the lot, on the road, and on the highway just to make it to the peace and serenity of the lightly traveled back roads to make it home to Harding. Trying to have as much time as possible before the wife and kids got home today, I didn't dare stop anywhere, even for gas. I did that on the weekends or in the mornings if I could. I got home, worked on our coal fire place, and booked it up to the mother-in-law's house to get the little kid.

Clara knew that today was dance day, so as soon as she heard the quad come up the hill, she was already waiting for me by the window. My mother-in-law's house had two big sliding glass doors that faced the driveway. Through one of them, I could see my little princess was with my mother-in-law's dog, Buddy. Buddy was already barking and growling at me. The dog was my mother-in-law's dachshund, and while he loved his girls, he hated me. I mean, he literally hated me; he barked at me and would tear me apart if he had the chance. I had no idea why. I had been nothing but nice to him. And I knew that dachshunds could be very aggressive and were generally not good with little kids, but while Clara beat up on him all day to his delight, when this bro saw me, *bam*, it was on.

Whatever. Before I had a chance to come in, Clara is already dressed and running out the door toward the quad.

"Hi, Clara!" I yelled as I headed toward the basement to work on the coal stove.

"Hi, Daddy. We going to dance class today?" she asked happily as she climbed into the quad.

"Yep, do you want to get a kid's meal for dinner?"

"Sure!"

"Okay, get in the quad, and I will work on Grandma's coal stove. I will be right out," I said as I opened the door to the basement. I filled up the coal hopper and emptied out the ashes. Momma Joyce was upstairs, so it only took me a few seconds to get this all taken care of before I left.

Clara and I made our way back down to the house just as Joyce was pulling into the driveway. Of course, Clara started jumping up and down in her seat, yelling, "Mommy, Mommy, Mommy is home! Hi, Mommm!"

Joyce parked her car under the carport as I waited for her to get into her spot. Once she was in her spot, I pulled up next to her, and she rolled down her window.

"Hi, Clara!"

"Hi, Mommm!"

Everyone got out of their vehicles and passed around the hugs and kisses.

"Hey, beautiful, how was your day?" I asked her as I took off my hat to give her a kiss.

"Good, but man, oh man, these kids are really bleeding me dry of my hand sanitizer," she said as she released me from a hug.

"What do you mean?" I asked.

"Remember how I got all that stuff yesterday?" she asked. "I went through almost an entire big bottle because all the kids needed their own hand sanitizer bottles refilled. All have the same story, 'My mom ran out' or 'We don't have any left at the house. Can I have some of yours?' And, *aaand*, the school's hand sanitizer sucks because it isn't alcohol based, so no one uses it. But of course, there is a ton of that stuff."

"Ugh, well, just make sure there is enough for what you need," I replied.

Joyce looked at me and said, "I will. Tonight is dance, right? Last week, when I took the girls, there were a lot less people. Are you taking the kids to get dinner out?"

"Yeah, do you want anything?" I asked, knowing that she probably would.

"If you are stopping on your way back home, can you get me some fries?" she asked me with another hug.

"Not a problem, Mrs. B," I said.

After I said that, the bus pulled up with Peanut on it. She hopped off it, knowing that today was dance class day and that we were getting dinner out. But first, she needed to get any of her homework done at the house before we left. I asked her to do that because if we had to do it at the dance studio, usually, the place was so packed in the waiting rooms with, well, mostly dance moms that there weren't any chairs to sit on. So we would have to do it in the cramped car in the cold. Clara's class was at 6:00 p.m. and went for half an hour, then we'd have to wait for Joyce's class to start at 7:00 p.m., which was also half an hour long. At least this year, their classes were on the same day. Last year, Joyce's class was on Thursdays while Clara's class was on Tuesdays, but that changed when Clara got older. So now, for the next few years, everyone was on the same day. Thank goodness!

With Joyce's homework done, everyone having gone potty, the coal stoves having been worked on, and everyone all packed up (which, by the way, why does it take half an hour to put on tutus and shoes and grab dance bags?), we got into the car. Between classes and dinner, the bill added up, so all this overtime that I was getting from working so much was going to help.

The kids got their kid's meals, and I got my salad. Who knew that drive-through had good salads? Up until my gallbladder surgery last year, I had no idea. After we picked up dinner, we headed over to the dance studio to eat in the car and wait for the classes.

"Whoa," I muttered to myself when I was pulling into the parking lot.

"What, Dad?" Joyce asked with a mouth full of french fries.

"Look! Look at all the open parking spots!" I exclaimed as we pulled into a near empty parking lot.

This place was normally packed with minivans, SUVs, and little kids running around the parking lot. There was not even half of that here tonight. I looked at the time on my phone—5:45 p.m. We were a little bit early, but normally, this place was hopping!

I found our normal spot at the backside of the building under a big oak tree and settled in. Joyce stayed in the car and went over her spelling words as I walked Clara around to the entrance of the building, and we both walked into the door. Normally, on a Thursday, there would be little toddlers crawling around on the floor; like, five hundred dance moms and maybe one or two dance dads all engaged on either their cell phones or talking and not paying attention to anyone else; and the receptionist handling barrage after barrage of questions from whoever—all packed into a tiny waiting room.

But tonight, it was like there was a blizzard outside and only the die-hards came in. There were maybe, *maybe*, a dozen moms huddled in their groups, chatting, and Ro, the receptionist, was just sitting there, fiddling around with some paperwork.

"Hey, guys!" said Ro as she saw us come in.

"Oh my god, Ro, what the heck is going on? Were they calling for any snow and people just didn't want to risk coming out here?" I asked.

"*Do you have my outfit!*" blurted out Clara.

Their dance recital was coming up in two and a half months. Back in January, the kids all got fitted for their outfits, and every time we had come in since then, Clara wanted to know where her dress was.

"No, sweetie, not yet. It's going to be another two or three weeks, sometime in mid-April, okay?" said Ro.

"Okay! Bye, Daddy!" said Clara gleefully as she bolted it into her dance room with her teacher and other dance friends.

"Bye, hon!" I said as I waved at her while she ran into her room. Then I turned back to the receptionist's desk and asked, "Okay, Ro, so what's going on?"

"Okay, so yeah, they weren't calling for snow or anything. I am hearing rumors, though, from what the parents were saying here last week, which was that a lot of people we were worried about what they said on the news about this virus quarantining ships and those nursing homes out in Washington State. Some of them are keeping their kids home until it gets a little safer. I don't know. It seems like a bunch of to-do to me," said Ro as she pointed to the TV in the corner, which had the news on.

"Yeah, I don't know either. But whatever, as long as their checks cleared at the beginning of the month, right, Ro!" I said, laughing as I headed out the door and back to the car to go over Joyce's spelling words with her.

"That's right. Okay, see you, Art," said Ro.

"Okay, Ro. See you in a few," I said as I closed the door behind me. We probably could have stayed in the waiting room, but why break routine, right?

The rest of the night went on as normal. I stayed in the car with Joyce, having my salad and reviewing her words until Clara's class was over. While we did that, I remembered that I hadn't called and talked to my brother in a while. My brother Brian and I got along great, and sometimes I missed him. Life had taken us on two different paths. While mine led me to stay near where we grew up (well, I mean, I lived two hours from where I grew up, but whatever), his life led him to the big city of Philadelphia. He was a construction manager down there, where he lived with his wife and two kids.

"Hey, Peanut, do you want to call Uncle Brian?" I asked.

"Yeaaah!" she screeched. Both kids loved Uncle Brian.

I turned on my phone and, through the Bluetooth, hooked it up to the car. And then I called my brother.

Ring, ring, ring.

"Yo," answered Brian.

"Yo, baby bro, how are you?" I said.

"Hi, Uncle Brian!" yelled Joyce.

"Hey, guys, how are you?" he asked.

"We're good, Uncle Brian. We're at dance class," said Joyce.

"You are? Awesome. Hi, Art. Or did you change your name yet? Elizabeth said you have less balls now than you did before, which is shocking, really," said Brian.

"Shut up. I'd say something different, but the kid is here. Anyway, how are you?" I said.

"Trying to work, but the stupid governor isn't making it easy for me," said Brian.

"Why?" I asked, puzzled.

"You know how the governor is only locking down certain parts of the state?" asked Brian.

"Nah, I really haven't paid much attention to that stuff," I said.

"Yeah, I guess I would be in shock too still if I didn't have my balls anymore." (Sidenote: how many people do not know how vasectomies work?) "But for those of us who still pay attention to the world around us, you know how the governor is shutting down or telling everyone to stay at home but only in certain parts of the state? Well, I can't get half of my work done because my construction sites are in one county, but if the county where my crews are from are shut down, they won't be coming into work. I have houses that have foundations built, but the framers and painters are from a county where they are scared to leave their houses. We're scrambling down here. It sucks, buddy," said Brian.

"Wait, so people are actually paying attention to what the governor is telling them to do? Or are they just genuinely scared of what this virus is?" I asked.

"I think its half and half. But whatever it is, our construction sites are slowing down, and I am wondering how much longer we can go before we're going to have to stop because I can't get these houses built," said Brian, obviously upset over what was going on.

"Hey, I have to go get Clara from her dance class. You be good down there, okay?" I said.

"Yeah, you too. Tell Joyce and Momma Joyce I said hi," he said.

"You too. Tell the wife and kids I said hi," I said. "Bye."

After I hung up, I went in and got Clara after she was done with her class and went back to the car, staying there until it was time for Joyce's class. Peanut was older and went in without me because she knew where her classroom was and who her teacher was. When it came time for Joyce's class to end, I went in with Clara to go get her like I normally did. In the winter, it was kind of dark out, and I didn't want her trying to run around the parking lot without me in case anything should happen, you know?

As Clara and I walked back into the waiting room, the owner, Bob, was at the desk, talking to Ro. The dance studio was owned by a married couple who were both teachers and were really nice people. It was part of the reason that we keep coming back every year.

"Hey, Bob," I said as I shook his hand.

"Art, hi! How are you?" he asked.

"I am doing okay. What is going on tonight, double your price on the classes or something?" I asked as Peanut came out into the waiting room.

"Art, I have no idea what's going on!" exclaimed Bob. "For the past two weeks, less and less people have been arriving for dance. People are not showing up for their classes. I have never seen anything like this."

"Is anyone pulling their kids out of classes or saying they aren't coming back?" I asked, sensing the oddly out-of-place concern coming from a man who I had never heard be sooo pessimistic and cautious.

"No, not yet, but this is really weird. I hope this doesn't last a long time because I don't know what we're going to do if this goes on for a few months, you know?" said Bob.

"Listen, Bob, the president of the United States would have to declare an emergency or something before I ever stop bringing my kids back to your classes!" I replied. "Don't worry, my checks will clear."

"I know, Art. They always do. See you next week," said Bob as he went back into one of the classrooms.

"See you! Okay, girls, ready to go home?" I asked both kids, who, at this point, were bored to tears.

"Yeah, but Dad, don't forget that you promised Mom fries," said Clara.

"I didn't forget. How could I forget about your mom!" I said.

We got into the car and made our way back home, making sure to stop for fries for Joyce—a large order of no-salt fries so they would be nice and fresh. The girls chatted away about class as my mind started to wander. I didn't bring them to class last week because of the surgery and had missed the class before that because of me getting a load of coal, so Joyce brought the kids. So three weeks ago was the last time I brought the kids. Everything was fine; literally everything was normal only three weeks ago. *So you're telling me that in three weeks, the world around us changed? Yeah, okay, buddy, calm down. You are overreacting.*

We walked into the door to the house. Joyce was relaxing on her recliner chair.

"Hey, beautiful, I got you something nice and hot. *Me!*" I said, hiding the fries behind my back.

"Uh-huh, that's nice. Where are my fries?" asked Joyce, grinning.

"Oh, and I got these for you too." I presented to her proudly my kill.

She smiled and took them as the girls ran past me up to their rooms to go play video games. I sat down on the sofa beside her as she watched something on TV.

"How was class tonight?" she asked.

"It was great," said Clara.

"Oh, did the girls dance nicely?"

"Oh, well, yeah, they danced nicely, but there was hardly any-one there," I said. "A lot of room in the waiting room, and no one trying to kill each other while getting in and out of the parking lot."

"You know, when I was there last week and the week before when you were getting coal and everything, I saw that a lot of peo-ple weren't showing up," said Joyce. "Did they cancel classes or something?"

"No, Bob said that it was people just not showing up. They paid for the classes, but they aren't bringing the kids. And Ro said she was overhearing from the dance moms in the waiting room that the parents are afraid of this virus going around, so I don't know. I told Bob that it was going to take an act of the president for us to stop coming."

Joyce became slightly more reserved in her chair when I was done talking.

"If something bad happens, I don't know about taking them, Artie. But up until then, yeah, go for it," said Joyce.

Chapter 6

Day 5

March 13, 2020, Friday

Beep, beep, beep.

I groggily rolled over and slapped my alarm clock off. It was my fifth day back at work, and man, did my crotch ache worse again! I sat up and looked over at Joyce. My god, she was more beautiful than yesterday. I leaned over and gave her a really light kiss on her exposed—oh, for Pete's sake, how was she lying now? Oh boy, it's her cheek this morning! "I love you, Joyce. Have a nice day at work." While it was Friday, I should be excited and happy, but given that we were mandated to work on Saturday, the thrill was all but gone. But there was always Sunday!

It was another ordinary day. All I thought about was what was going to happen as I got ready to go to work. I made another ordinary pot of coffee. I got my lunch into my lunch box. Anything exciting? Nope, just my usual salad, which I had been eating every day since I got back to work after my gallbladder surgery last year.

"Good morning, boys. You guys be good for Joyce when she wakes up, okay?" I said to Buster and Shaggy as I walked out of the mudroom onto the deck. It was another cold, ordinary day—literally. This morning started out like every morning so far with the noticeable exception that we were much busier at work than we should be at this time of year.

I got into my truck and started my ordinary ride into work, and as soon as I turned on my radio and my favorite talk radio station came on, broadcasting out of Pittston up by Interstate 81, I knew something was up.

"The markets took a big hit yesterday as coronavirus worries abound when on Wednesday, the World Health Organization declared an official pandemic. The Dow Jones closed at 21,085 on Thursday, a far cry from 29,523 that it was at literally a month ago today. The weather forecast for today…" The announcer trailed off as I got really excited really quickly and lost focus on the rest of the broadcast. The part about the stock market got to me, though.

See, about two years ago, I enrolled into our company's stock purchase plan. Every week, the company took 3 percent out of my pay and put it into an account at a brokerage firm to be used twice a year to buy company stocks at a 5 percent discounted rate. When I first enrolled, the company stock was doing great, but my 3 percent didn't really buy me too much. But about two weeks after the first purchase date, the stock price tanked, which, normally, I wouldn't care, but I caught all kinds of heck from Joyce, who would ask every day, "How is your stock doing Art?" knowing full well that I bought it at $108 a share and that it dropped to about $44 a share. Sooo if the economy was tanking and our stock price went down, and since our next stock purchase date was at the end of March, hurray! I would be able to pick up a lot of stocks at a bargain price! What the heck was that thing about the World Health Organization declaring a pandemic or whatever? I don't know. I am sure I would have heard something if it was that serious.

The road going up to the warehouse was unusually busy, and as I got closer to our building, I saw why: trucks—I mean, lots of trucks. Trucks actually backed up the road going to the truck entrance. The employee entrance was a bit before that entrance, so I had to squeeze in between the line. But wow, that meant it was busy. At least those in the weekend shift was here this morning, and Calieb, the weekend-shift supervisor, was there to help Jim.

Walking into the building, I noticed that all the forklifts were being used, sooo great. That meant that I would not have one to use until those in the third shift left. I clocked in and started walking down the docks to the office when I noticed Calieb actually on a forklift, apparently doing trucks.

"Yo, Calieb, you okay?" I asked as he slowed down when he saw me.

"Whyyy?" asked my puzzled-looking coworker.

"Why are you doing trucks?" I asked as I tried to avoid being hit by all the other forklift operators who were just tearing up and down the docks, honking their horns—well, as fast as you could tear something up at eight miles per hour.

He looked kind of shocked at me, like how did I not know?

"We are sooo far behind. How did you not know?" he asked.

"Well, I knew we were busy, but inventory is always busy. Doesn't matter how many trucks we have, there is always someone screwing up something that I have to fix," I said, laughing, but then I stopped when I saw that he wasn't laughing.

"Did you read your text from Big Boss?" he asked.

I took out my phone and didn't see one.

"I don't have one. Why?" I responded and showed him my phone.

"You guys are mandated the entire weekend. Everyone is," said Calieb.

"*What!*" I exclaimed

"Yeah, so buckle up, buttercup. Your shift isn't going to be happy," he said as he drove away.

"Why does everyone say it's my shift? I am not the supervisor!" I yelled but was pretty confident that (a) he already knew that or (b) didn't care.

I walked into the office, and the weekend-shift dispatcher was working with Jim. They were both extremely busy, talking loudly with drivers as everyone was trying to get to their loads. I had a pile of notes on my desk—missing, missing, damaged, lost, wrong item number, wrong lot date, and on and on. When we had a first-shift lead coordinator, it was lot better to work through these problems because I could focus on these and resolve them quickly. But he went to another building "temporarily," leaving us with no supervisor or lead. So everything just kind of fell on me because, as the inventory guy, I had been here the longest and knew more of the system than anyone on the floor. I sat down at my desk and started to work.

As normal, Big Boss came in at about five minutes before the first shift started.

"Yo, what is going on with what Calieb told me?" I asked as he walked by.

He stopped at my desk with a serious look that I didn't normally attribute to his easygoing yet well-thought-out normal demeanor and said, "We are going to be hit with more juice than ever before in our history. We are not staffed for this, we know. There are going to be complainers, we know. I will do the preshift meeting with you. Until we can get ahead of all this, we have to mandate every day ten hours minimum until further notice."

"Even me? Are we going to have enough forklifts?" I asked because normally, when they mandated, I could come in on the weekends because there was a lift. During the weekdays, when they mandated, it didn't apply to the office staff or inventory because there would not be enough forklifts.

"Yes, even if there is no forklift, you can at least help out the office," said Big Boss.

"You got it, boss," I said.

Before we had our meeting, I texted Joyce really quick:

> Hey, beautiful, was just told that I am working 10 hour days and weekends until further notice starting tomorrow. I don't know what exactly is going on, but I love you very much. And I am sorry I won't be as home as much for a while.

I knew that she wouldn't get this message until after a few hours, so I put my phone in my pocket and headed out the office door to do the preshift with Big Boss.

Telling everyone that we were all mandated to work every day for ten hours a day until further notice went as well as you pretty much figured it would. Some folks just nodded their heads while others outright said they would be calling off. A lot of people wanted to know why a weekend shift wasn't mandated. Big Boss said that it was because we didn't have enough forklifts, which was fine. I was not sad about that.

That pretty much set the tone for the rest of the day. Around noon, I did get a text from Joyce informing me of what happed at the World Health Organization:

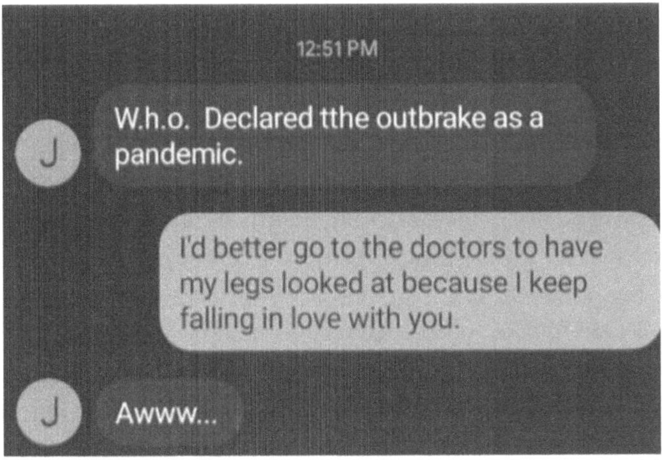

After that, Joyce did not respond to my texts, which could either be good or bad. She had a very old cell phone that did not have a long battery life, so either it might be dead, she was angry that I had to work all weekend, she had the ringer off and didn't know that I was trying to contact her, or whatever. I was just worried about getting to the house in time for when Peanut got off the bus starting next week because I would be getting out at exactly 3:00 p.m., which didn't give me a lot of time to go from Mountain Top to Harding and be home before the bus got there. Joyce and I would just have to work that out.

At 2:00 p.m., my shift ended. I walked out to my truck, dodging the nightmarish race of tractor trailers going around the building either trying to leave or get to their doors to be worked. It seemed no longer like organized chaos; it was just plain and simple chaos.

At first I didn't have the energy to turn on the radio, so I just got in my truck and started out at the employee gate to get home. When I got down to I-81 and headed north, I turned on the radio, expecting to hear a show host talking about politics, but instead, it was just very hurried and excited voices that were coming out of the speakers. It wasn't until a few minutes after the radio was on that the commotion began to make sense. And it was not good.

"As was stated moments ago," the guy on the radio said, "and, folks, we promise to keep everyone as up-to-date as possible with what information we are getting here in the newsroom, but the president of the United States has just declared a national state of emergency in response to the growing threat from the COVID-19 pandemic. In addition, the state governor, who, up until this point, had been closing down counties reporting outbreaks, has now announced that all nonessential businesses, government work, and schools will be shut down for a minimum of two weeks. All school districts in the state of Pennsylvania will be dismissing for their last time for at least two weeks at the end of the day today."

My heart stopped. Oh my god, *what*! What, what, what! I immediately started calling Joyce's number, and it went right to voice mail, which meant the battery was dead. I wasn't going to try to call the school because her and the other teachers might be trying to coordinate with what the district was going to do, so I needed to let her be a professional. But oh my god, my wife and baby were in the school! What the hell was going on?

As soon as I got home, I didn't worry about our coal stove or dinner. I got into the buggy and shot right up to Momma Joyce's house. I sped up her driveway, and when I got up there, Clara was already coming out. Momma Joyce poked her head out and yelled, "You take her home to her mom, and I will talk to you guys at a better time!" She didn't even let me get a word in while I gave Clara the biggest, tightest hug I ever had.

"I love you, Clara," I said to her as I pulled her hood up on her jacket.

"I love you too daddy!!!! We go home now?" she asked as she got into the quad.

But I still had to work on the coal stove. Clara waited for me as I ran. It only took me a few minutes as I rushed through the motions, but when I got back, I jumped into the quad and went back down the driveway. As we went down the mountain, I could see that Joyce's car was coming up the road and turning into our driveway. I couldn't wait to get to her. What had happened at school? Was she okay? Was there a plan for Peanut and the other kids?

She parked the car under the carport, and I pulled up next to her. She opened her door, looking right as me as I opened my door while looking right at her. We exited our vehicles at the same time and reached out for each other. I gave her a kiss on the forehead and whispered, "It's going to be okay, Joyce. In fact, have I had a chance to tell you today that you are the most beautiful woman in the world and that I am so happy that I married you?"

While still hugging me, she pulled back and bit and said, "I love you too, Arthur."

"If you want me to, I will resign from my position right now and stay home with you and the kids to be safe."

She smirked a bit. "What would happen if you did that?"

"Well, at some point, we would wonder how we were going to pay the bills," I said with a smile.

"No, I mean at work," she said.

"Well…" I had to think for a second. "There is already no supervisor or lead on the shift and no one to cover if I didn't come in. All the inventory issues would build up to the point that they probably would affect or stop some parts of the operations. There would be no one there to help the operators if something goes wrong. The building would probably shut down after a few weeks because there wouldn't be enough people to handle everything, and the people already there would be overwhelmed. I am not saying that the world would stop without me, but everyone who can go to work needs to be there."

Joyce, as loving as any wife could be, was very understanding. "You need to go to work. You work in food distribution, and when I went grocery shopping the other day, I had told Clara that it might be the last time we go grocery shopping for a while. It was nuts.

There were parts of the shelves being emptied, and I kind of had a sense that something bad was going to happen. Unless martial law is declared or I do not feel it is safe for you to go for whatever reason, you need to keep going to work."

I hugged her one more time. The sky was gray, it was cold, and it being March in Northeastern Pennsylvania, everything was all still kind of dead—no new life for another month or so. It might have seemed very soggy, cold, and depressing to anyone outside our bubble, but at that moment, despite what was literally happening around us, I felt safe and warm in the arms of the most beautiful woman I have ever known.

While we were hugging, the bus pulled up. I looked at Joyce then looked over at the bus to see Peanut hopping down the steps and heading across the street to Joyce and me. I motioned to the bus driver to hold on and not go away as I stepped into the bus. His name was Dave, a very nice person that we have known for years. He was an older guy with white hair and a white mustache and always wore denim.

"Hey, Dave, how is it going?" I asked with my hand outstretched to shake his hand.

"Oh, you know," he said with a shrug. "What do you think about what is going on?"

"I don't know about anyone else," I said. "But if the government is shutting everything down, the kids are going to be out of school longer than two weeks, I'll tell you that much."

"Yeah, I thought the same thing. You guys be good, okay?" he asked.

"Dave," I said, looking at him, knowing that there was a chance that I may not see this man for a veeerryyy long time, "you be careful, and take good care of yourself and the missus."

"Okay, guy, see you later," he said as I stepped off the bus.

When I got back to the driveway, Joyce was hugging both of the girls. Peanut broke away to give me a hug. *"Hi, Daddy! They closed school!"*

"Yeah, hon. I think they may have closed a lot of things! Listen, get your stuff inside, and we will make dinner." I glanced back and saw that Joyce's car was full of stuff. I reached out to help her as she started unloading some bags and boxes.

"I took some stuff home from my classroom. They didn't tell us that we had to clean out our rooms, but I don't know, Artie. I think this is going to be worse than what they think it is going to be. The district superintendent was going to be at a meeting with a couple of other superintendents from other school districts to talk about what was going on."

"What did they say at the school district?" I asked.

"I got two emails today. In the first email, we were told that we were going to be shut down for five days, and then half an hour later, the governor announced he was closing down the schools for ten days. Can you help me unload the car?" asked Joyce.

"Not a problem, hon," I said. "Let's get this stuff in the house and start dinner. The kids seem hungry."

After unpacking the car, while Joyce made dinner, Peanut worked on some homework at the kitchen table, and I worked on the coal stove. After that, I went upstairs where Joyce had the news on in the background. Reports were coming in of fights breaking out at grocery stores as supplies were being stressed. Standing in front of the TV, I watched this and muttered, "Well, I guess that explains that."

"Explains what?" Joyce said as she looked up from getting dinner ready. We were going to have pizza.

"Did you get my text?" I asked.

"No, why?"

"This morning we got mandated seven days a week until further notice. But if people are starting to hoard everything, that is probably why all of this week, we have been moving a lot of juice."

Joyce's demeanor got slumped, and the expression on her face was one of "You have got to be kidding me."

"How long is that going to be, until further notice?"

"I don't know. I really don't. Definitely this weekend, probably next weekend, but I don't know."

I went over and hugged Joyce again. Here we were, literally two people on completely opposite sides of the spectrum. Her work and the school district that she loved so much to teach at were literally stopping while I may not have a day off for weeks. After we stopped hugging, I took out my phone.

"What are you doing?" asked Joyce.

"I have to do something really quick," I said.

I took this moment to put on my social media page a message to all my co-workers, and the world:

March 13 at 3:45 p.m.

> To all my coworkers, these will be trying times. We work in the supply chain for the nation's food distribution network. I get it, working 7 days a week will be difficult. But hopefully, we can take stock in the fact that our efforts go beyond the appreciation of our customers and bosses but are vital to holding the nation together. You can complain all you want during our normal busy season, but the president of the United States just declared a national emergency. This is bigger than anything we have ever faced. We must prevail.

"Hey, Mom, can you help me?" asked little Joyce as she was just finishing up with her last question on her homework.

"I can help you, sweetie. What do you have?" I said as I walked over to the kitchen table to see what was wrong. I helped her along in time for dinner to be served. Clara and Peanut carried on a conversation about toys or video games, completely oblivious to the world, while Joyce and I were fixated on the television. The president was talking about the response the country would have to combat the "kung flu" problem, which was not really a problem, in his opinion, as it would go away on its own and on and on.

"Yeah, I don't have a whole lot of confidence in what this guy is saying," I said while eating.

"Me neither. So everyone has to go to work?" asked Joyce.

"Yeah, and we're supposed to work ten-hour days during the week," I said. "The problem is, there is no supervisor on the shift, so who or how is anyone going to pay attention the mandatory overtime thing? We aren't even staffed where we should be for this. Heck, we don't have enough people for the work we already do have! Hey, also, your mom said she would talk to us when there was time, it didn't have to be right now, about what's going on."

"Okay, you might want to give your mom and dad a call too."

"Yeah, you're right. Did anyone tell Mom thank you for dinner?" I asked as the girls had quieted down.

"Thanks for dinner, Mom," we all said in unison.

"You're welcome, guys," said Joyce. "Hey, do you think it would be a good idea to fill up all the cars and gas cans just in case something goes wrong with the gas stations?"

At first I thought it was a joke, but she was serious. I guess there was no more room at the moment for joking.

"Good thinking. Does anyone want to go with Dad to gas station?" I asked the kids as we started cleaning up our dinner plates.

"How about the girls stay and help Mom clean up, and Dad goes the gas station?"

"Buuut, Mom, we wanted to go with Dad," moped Clara.

I thought about what Joyce had said, and she was right. We now seriously had to consider what the kids were going to be exposed to.

"No, your mom's right, girls. You stay here, and Dad will go out."

I gave Joyce a kiss and took all the car keys. We kept her mom's car down at our house because the driveway was so awful. I went out to the shed, got the gas cans, put them in the back of the truck, and headed up the literal only gas station in Harding that was about ten minutes away. When I got there, apparently, I was not the only person with the same idea. The gas station only had four pumps, and each pump had someone in it right now, doing the same thing I was. So I waited and waited, and eventually, it was my turn. The people around me were friendly, smiling and saying hello, but it was a guarded type of stance they all had. After filling the truck and the gas cans, my twenty-five-minute trip took almost an hour.

I was putting away the gas cans when Joyce came out of the house and said, "What took you so long?"

"I guess we're not the only ones with the same ideas. There was a little bit of a line. I have to do your car and your mom's, and then I will take a shower because I am dirty."

"Yeah, you are, boy. Okay, I will watch the kids," said Joyce.

She went back into the house while I ventured out to continue filing up the cars. It was another wait in the line for my Joyce's car and then another wait in the line for her mom's car. This day was getting longer and longer by the second, ugh. This whole task was taking a little over an hour and a half to complete.

Once I was done parking all the cars, I went back into the house where Joyce was getting the kids' bike helmets and some kites.

"Do you want to go to the park, Daddy?" asked Joyce.

I saw what Joyce was doing for the kids and said yes. I was tired, I was filthy, and I wanted to lie down, but I got the bikes out of the shed and put them in the back of my truck as Joyce got the girls ready to go. We probably wanted to get over there before it got too dark.

We headed toward Frances Slocum State Park. It was a smaller-sized state park in the county that was named after a little girl who was abducted by Native Americans and became a Native American herself, then somehow, they named a park after her. The whole story was kind of hazy. If you were really interested, you should look into it.

Because we had bikes *and* kites, I knew of a parking area that would be perfect for both. We pulled into one of the more empty parking lots and parked. As Joyce and the kids got out of the truck, I got out the bikes out.

"Why did we park here?" asked Joyce.

I pointed to the field that was next to the parking lot. Beyond the field was the tree line for the forest where sometimes I took the kids for hikes. "The wind is blowing pretty good through the tree line over there, and we have a good spot to watch the kids ride their bikes in case they don't want to try and fly kites," I said.

"Good idea. Okay, girls, who wants to do to what?" asked Joyce.

The kids started yelping about what they wanted to do, and Joyce and I did our best to accommodate them. I helped get the kites flying and then passed them off to Mom and Peanut. Clara wanted to ride her bike, so I set her up, stood by the truck, and just kind of watched everything.

"Get on over here, Pa!" yelled Joyce, flying her kite.

"I'm coming, Ma!" I yelled back as I watched her and Clara.

"Don't worry about Clara. There is no traffic here. Come on, stand by me," said Joyce. "I won't bite."

"What if I asked you too?" I asked.

"Yeah, still wouldn't. Thanks for coming out here with me. I know you're beat. I just thought it would be nice to bring everyone out here to get their minds off things."

"It's okay, we all had a rough day. I can bring the girls out here more often to get them out of the house and give you a breather for the next two weeks if you want me to."

"I don't know, Artie, about that. What happens if everyone has the same idea as you, and they all come out at once? What would be the point of locking everything down if everyone still comes out and gathers anyway?" asked Joyce.

"I promise you that if we come out here and there are too many people, we will go right home," I replied.

She smiled and said okay. We enjoyed the rest of our time there as a family. When it was getting too dark to see, Joyce and I gathered up the kids and our stuff. I got the bikes back into the truck, and we all headed home. When we got home, though, Joyce wanted the kids and everyone to take a bath.

We unpacked the truck, and Joyce got the kids and herself upstairs for baths and showers. When everyone was near done, I patiently waited for them to finish up before stepping into the bathroom to take my shower. As Joyce finished drying off the kids, she was putting their clothes in the laundry basket when I came up behind her and gave her a hug.

"Hey, care to join me and save water?" I said with a smirk.

"Yeah, right, you wish! Get your dirty hands off my clean shirt and get cleaned up."

"I'll get you one of these days!" I said to her as she was exiting the bathroom.

"Joyce. *Hey*, Joyce, wait. I have to get up early tomorrow. Do you want the kids to go to bed with me, or what do you want to do?"

"When were you going to take them to bed?"

I looked at the clock, and it was almost 8:30 p.m.

"Probably when I'm done with my shower. It's getting late."

"I will let them sleep in the living room tonight because there is no school. You go ahead to sleep. I love you."

"Well, with that logic, I guess they can sleep in the living room for a few weeks!" I said back. "Hey, Joyce, have I had a chance to tell you today that I think you are the most beautiful woman in the world and that I love you?"

"Love you too, Artie."

Chapter 7

Day 6: The First Weekend

March 14, 2020, Saturday

Beep, beep, beep.

God, did I hate that alarm clock. I rolled over to give Joyce a quick kiss on her exposed—wait, what? I felt around, and no Joyce! I got up out of bed, and as I walked down the hallway toward the bathroom, I saw that the TV in Peanut's room was on. When I walked in, it was a cute yet heartbreaking sight: Joyce was in the bed with both the girls, who had both cuddled around their mom. Normally, we let the kids sleep in the same bed on special occasions like weekends or long holidays and in the wintertime too when it got really cold. If one got out of bed and went to snuggle with the other, we didn't normally stop them because they would be breaking into our room and trying cuddle with us if we didn't! I guessed sometime during the night, Joyce put both the girls to bed and must've dozed off with them. More often than not, I put the kids to bed, but I got the impression that a lot of routines were going to change for the time being.

On the drive into work, the only thing on the talk radio was updates about the virus—what states were doing what, the number of people infected, the number of people who died in each state, what the federal government was doing to help the states deal with their outbreaks, etc. It seemed like every second that the radio was on, though, there was a special breaking-news report. I mean, literally, every other thought from the talk show host was about a new, imminent danger that they were going to have to issue a special report on.

As I pulled into the employee parking lot, there were only two or three open spaces. The rest were jammed. So we had third-shift, first-shift, some of second-shift guys, and weekend-shift operators here—aaawesome. As I parked my car and put on my safety vest, I saw Kurt exiting his vehicle about five spaces down.

"Hey, Kurt!"

"Good morning, Mr. Art. How are we doing on this fine Saturday morning?" he asked as we both headed into building and up to the time clock.

"I don't know, Kurt. What the hell is going on, man!" I exclaimed.

"I know. What's going to happen to Joyce and your daughter?" asked Kurt.

"Well, it's the damnedest thing, Kurt. Joyce was told yesterday that they are closing down the school for just a week, then it's two weeks. She doesn't think that it's going to be just two weeks either. It's going to be a lot longer. So at the same time that she is being told that she needs to stop going to work, you and I are told we don't know when the mandated overtime is going to stop. Ain't that something?" I asked as I opened the door to the building.

We both laughed as we clocked in and went to find a forklift.

Looking at all the doors that were opened with forklifts going in and out of them, I knew that there was no way that there was going to be a forklift available for me. After a few minutes of searching, I gave up and started heading toward the shipping office. It was a tornado of activity where I was walking too. People were going in and out of the office, getting paperwork to do their trucks, and having problems with the system, and in the middle of it was Calieb.

"Good morning, team," I said as I walked up to Calieb.

He didn't look that thrilled to me. "What did you just say?" asked Calieb.

"Ummm, good morning. *Hey, watch it!*" I exclaimed as someone ran into my back.

"My bad. I just need to get more seals for my trucks," replied the weekend-shift operator.

The operator darted into the office and then back out as Calieb went back to his computer screen and said, "So do you not see what's going on around here right now? Are we sure that we want to call it a good morning?"

"Well, listen, I don't have a forklift, so what do you need me to do?" I asked as I walked over to my desk and fired up my computer.

Calieb immediately handed me a long list of things that he hadn't been able to address. They were some of the issues the he couldn't get to, and I was not going to be able to completely get to either. But there were other issues that I could fix. Incorrect lot dates, locations showing "out of service" in the system that needed to be put back into service, problems with a whole bunch of orders in the system, and other challenges were what I concentrated on. While I worked on the tasks that Calieb had handed to me, I turned on my walkie-talkie radio to see if anyone was having problems they needed help with on the floor.

When someone had a problem that needed help from the office, I fielded as many as I could. Pallet tags that appeared to be dead that needed research, directions on how to process damage on the floor, help with a problem in the case-pick area—most of these problems I could help with because I had been with the juice company for ten years in almost every nonmanagement position imaginable besides sanitation and maintenance. When the operators heard my voice on the radio, they started directing their questions to me instead of Calieb, which freed him up to work with the truck drivers.

Most of the day was like that, and while normally, there were would be brief pauses of downtime, no one in the office had time to chat or nibble on lunch. Every now and then, I left my computer to go on the floor and help with either picking up pallets or guiding someone through on the computer screen. Just leaving my desk every now and then was nice. The busyness definitely helped the ten hours go by quicker.

As the end of the day approached, I left the office to go to the bathroom, and I noticed that after those in the third shift had left, there was actually a forklift or two available.

"Yo, Calieb!" I yelled from outside the office. "There are forklifts available. Do you want me to do a truck before I go?"

"Listen, it's up to you," said Calieb. "But it would definitely help us out if you would."

"You got it, buddy. Just let me hit the John, and then I will jump on trucks," I said.

I did my business and then got the paperwork for the truck I would do before I went home. It was an outbound trailer going to a big box retailer. Now, when I load my trailers, I load the tall, heavy product in the front and the low and light in the back. It had to do with how the trailer would weigh and scale tickets and a lot of other boring, mundane stuff that mostly no one reading this book outside of transportation would appreciate. But because I used to drive trucks to pay my way through grad school (yeah, I had my CDL), I knew how I would have appreciated a truck being loaded, so I did it for the next guy. Inventory karma, ya know?

I got my paperwork, and almost immediately, I was having problems. Pallets were either stuck up in the racking or were missing from their assigned locations and were actually a few locations downwind. Normal operators would just skip over them, but because I knew that at some point or another, Mark or I would be dealing with them anyway, I would take a few extra minutes and fix the problems as I went along. I was doing inventory *and* operations stuff at the same time. *Boom*—I just justified my paycheck, y'all!

I finished working on my truck just as the rest of the guys on second shift who didn't come in earlier started to arrive. I walked into the office with my paperwork in my hand, giving it to Calieb to file, and I noticed that even though it was insanely busy and we were all working ourselves into an early grave, he didn't seem fatigued, really.

"Still up for some more, eh, Calieb? Not that tired?" I asked.

"The day goes by so fast you don't have a chance to be tired. Going to see you tomorrow?" asked Calieb.

"Yeah, you will. Have a nice day, team," I said as I grabbed my lunch box from my desk and left the office.

"See you, Art," was the reply.

As I drove out of the parking lot with the rest of those in the same shift, I kind of wondered how long were we going to be mandated to work every day. Who on earth was buying all this juice? I mean, I am not complaining because I don't normally get overtime in the winter, but this was going to be nuts.

I also thought about my mom and dad. I didn't call them last night. They lived out in Pike County on the New York state line—about an hour and a half away from me. They lived in the house that they brought up my brother, sister, and I in.

"Well, now is as good a time as any," I said as I started bringing them up on the computer screen in my truck. The Bluetooth kicked on, and I heard the ringing.

"Hi, Honey," said Mom. At the same time, I heard the other phone in my parents' house pick up. It was my dad.

"Hi, Arty."

"Hi, Mom, Dad. How are you guys doing?" I asked.

"Well, we're stuck in the house because they are making the president lock everything down!" said Mom.

"Mom, it's a global pandemic. I think he is doing this for the best of everyone," I said.

"I think it's a way to make the president lose the election," said Mom.

"How is work?" asked Dad. "Are you guys still open?"

"Yeah, Dad, I have no idea what's going on, but the amount of juice leaving the building is biblical. I have never seen this much stuff leave so quickly in my ten-some-odd years of doing this. We are already mandated to work ten-hour days, and we got mandated to work this weekend too," I said.

"It's that busy, huh? Really? Is there any kind of particular juice that's leaving, or is it just that everything that can go is going?" asked Dad.

"Whatever we have is being sold right now. We are actually emptying the building!" I said excitedly.

"Oh my god," said Mom. "Is everyone safe where you are? Is everyone okay?"

"Yeah, Mom, we're good. Joyce had a bad feeling about what was going on in the news, so on the last grocery trip she went on, she got *a ton* of food. We'll be okay for a few weeks," I replied.

"Yeah, we were just at the grocery store too, and we have lots of food and supplies. It should last us a pretty long time," said Mom.

"Well, that's good," said Dad. "All righty, Art, I am going to lie down. I will talk to you later. I love you," said Dad.

"All right, Dad, I will talk to you later. Mom, I am close to my house. I will let you go too," I said, about to hang up the phone.

"All right, sweetie. I love you too. Tell Joyce and the girls that we said hi and that we know this is all going to blow over in a little while. I will talk to you later," said my mom as she hung up the phone.

I got home, and while it wasn't terribly cold out, it was still brisk. Joyce was sitting on a chair on the porch, waiting for me.

"Hey, beautiful," I said as I opened up the gate to the porch and plopped myself down onto the chair next to her. "Have I had a chance to tell you that I think that you are the most beautiful woman in the world and that I am so happy that I married you?"

"I love you too," she said, smiling at me.

"How was your day?" I asked.

"It was good. The school is sending out emails to the teachers about what's going to happen and how we are going to keep teaching," she said as I took and held her hand.

"Oh, wow, really that's great! What is the plan?" I asked.

"Well, there isn't a really cohesive one right now," she said, sighing.

"Oh, that's good," I snarkily replied.

"I think they are planning on using online classrooms, but I don't know if it's going to work. Not everyone in the district has access to the Internet. I am guessing that they were trying to plan for something like this over the past few days, but who would have ever thought that we would be shutting down schools during a pandemic!"

Just at that second, Peanut popped her head out of the door.

"Daddy!" she yelled excitedly.

"Hey, princess, were you and your sister good for your Mom today?" I asked.

"Yes!" she said.

"Yeah, they were pretty good," confirmed Joyce.

"Daddy, do you want to play with me?" asked Peanut.

While part of me was like, "Kid, do you not see that I am exhausted?" the other part of me was like, "How do I say no to my little princess?"

"Sure, sweetie, what do you want to do?" I asked.

"Ummm, can wc play badminton?" she said as she held up a racket.

Joyce liked playing tennis on her game system, and during the summer months, we would bring out the badminton set and play every now and then. But it's definitely different now because it's cold. I shrugged it off and said, "Did you get out the birdies and a few rackets?"

She held out her other hand that did indeed have birdies and rackets.

"What a great idea. Let's go to the other side of the house, and I will watch you and Dad play from the porch swing," said Joyce as she nudged me with her elbow. I know, I know. Dad needed to play with the kids.

"Okay, let me take off my work boots and put on my sneakers."

Everyone shuffled into the house and headed to the other side where the yard was flatter to play badminton. On the other side of the house, we also had a porch swing set up where occasionally, Joyce and I would spend a few minutes to watch traffic on the corner lot and talk. Joyce settled onto the swing with her tablet while I grabbed a big tree branch to use as a makeshift divider for Joyce and I to hit over like a net, only it was a log.

Little Joyce, her racket in hand, went to the other side of the log, and we started to play badminton. It took her a couple of swings to hit the birdie, but after she did, we started bouncing it back and forth. I personally liked playing this game. In fact, before we had kids, Joyce and I used to play it all the time.

We had played for a good hour before she started complaining about being cold. We picked up our stuff, I put the branch next to the porch swing, and I sat down next to wife Joyce. She was doing something peculiar. She was just looking up into the sky.

"Have you been doing that the whole time while we were playing?" I asked quizzically.

Joyce looked over at me with this sort of grim demeanor. "Look," she said, pointing toward the sky above where were playing.

I watched in awe as I saw a line of airplanes thousands of feet in the sky, all heading east and southeast. There were five that I could see, but while they moved across the sky, as one disappeared over the eastern horizon, a new one appeared over the western horizon. With Wilkes-Barre Scranton International Airport being only half an hour away, it was not unusual to see a plane or two every day, but this was totally different. The jets were bigger, and they were flying much higher.

"Oh my god," I said as I watched with Joyce. I grabbed her hand.

"Where do you think they are all going?" thought Joyce out loud.

"Well, they are heading east, sort of southeast. That way, if you weren't flying international, I guess you would be heading to New York City or Newark."

"What about Philly?" asked Joyce.

"Philadelphia is directly south of here. They would have to make a sharp turn, but they are all flying in a straight line from horizon to horizon. So I don't think so. Where do you think they are all going?" I asked.

"I think that everyone in all the other countries are trying to get out. We just shut everything down, like, locally, schools, restaurants, and whatever. We didn't shut down the airlines. So maybe they figured that they better get out now while they can," said Joyce.

I just sat there and watched the show with her.

"Where is Clara?" I asked, wondering where she was because I haven't seen her in the hours since I got home. But of course, like clockwork, from inside the house, we heard her scream, "*But Joooyccceee!*"

"Does that answer your question?" asked Joyce as we both kept on watching the planes fly over our heads.

"Yep," I replied with a tinge of resignation in my voice.

"You have to work tomorrow, right?" asked Joyce.

"Yep," I said.

"For how long?" asked Joyce.

"I'm not quite sure, but it might be for a bit. Who knows how many weekends this is going to take? But, Joyce, have I had a chance to tell you that you are the most beautiful woman in the world and that I am so happy that I married you?" I asked Joyce as I leaned in for a kiss.

"I love you too," she replied as she kissed me.

"*Claraaa, nooo, that's mine!*" is what we heard next from inside the house, followed by a crash and a couple of thuds.

"I reckon this is going to be one long pandemic," said Joyce as she got up from the porch swing.

"Yea me, too."

Day 7

March 15, 2020, Sunday

Beep, beep, beep.

God, did I hate that alarm clock. I rolled over to give Joyce a quick kiss on her exposed arm this time. I got up for work, but along with my coffee, which I usually made, I decided that I was going to need a little extra something to keep me going because I was starting to feel a little drained of energy. I didn't normally work this many hours, and while the overtime was great, I made an egg sandwich to help move me along.

On the ride into work, I left the radio off and just drove in silence. All I wanted to do was take a short break from all the breaking-news alerts and drive. As I got closer to the warehouse, the new normal was taking root as the number of trucks waiting to be worked was more than the previous day. Somehow, this had all got to slow down.

When I punched into work, I saw that there were no available forklifts. Go figure. As I started walking down toward the shipping office, I continued to notice something about the warehouse that seemed, well, off. I had gotten used to all the unexpected busyness that was going all around us, but I noticed that the top level of all the racking was empty. Empty? Empty? How? During the normal year, in February through about April, the warehouse would get really full of juice to prepare for the summer rush. We should be struggling to walk around without tripping over the stuff, but now I was looking at row after row of empty top-level shelves. What was going on now?

"What are you looking at there, Mr. Art? Trying to find heaven?"

I turned around and saw Kurt getting into the last available forklift.

"I don't know what you mean there, Kurt. Look around. With all the overtime we're getting, *this* is heaven!" I said as we both laughed. "No, but seriously, have you taken a look up in the racks lately?"

Kurt took a look up, and I saw the expression on his face. He knew *exactly* what I was talking about.

"You know, I haven't even noticed. Look at all these open locations!" said Kurt.

"You getting a bad feeling like me?" I asked.

"I've been doing this for years, and I have never seen the warehouse like that at this time of year. That's not right. That's not right. That should be full!" said Kurt.

"I am going to check something out in the office when I get a chance," I said as I started walking to the office once again.

"I know you'll take care of it!" said Kurt as he took off on his forklift and started working.

I walked into the shipping office, and it was once again semiorganized chaos. I sat down at my desk and logged in. While I did not have access to all the reports that I could ever want, the inventory people did have access to some of the basic operation reports. The ones that I wanted to see was what the inbound schedule looked like versus the outbound schedule.

Basically, in warehousing, because we weren't the producing plant, we didn't actually make anything. The logic behind how we were set up was this: instead of a massive plant that made juice and had room to store it, they used all the space to make production lines and then built warehouses around the plant to store and ship the product.

"What are you looking at?" asked Calieb while he was walking by.

"I wanted to see what our outbounds and inbounds are looking like for the week ahead," I said as I looked at my dual monitors.

"Why, the outbound schedule has been changing every hour lately. It's almost impossible to tell what your week is looking like. Don't worry. You're probably going to be working overtime for a while," replied Calieb.

"That isn't why I wanted to know," I said as I pointed out the window of the office into the warehouse.

Calieb looked up and saw the same thing that Kurt and I saw.

"Wow, look at that," replied Calieb.

I peered over the two reports and pretty quickly found my answer. "Look, here," I said. "You're right. It's hard to peg down how many outbounds are going to be added for the week, but it's not even Monday. And we are looking at close to five hundred outbound trucks, not including what they are going to add on. But look at the inbounds. Monday, twenty, Tuesday, thirty, Wednesday, fifteen, Thursday, forty-five, Friday, fifty. Nothing for Saturday or Sunday yet."

"Sooo sooner or later, it won't matter how many outbound we have on the schedule. Half of them we won't be able to load because we're going to run out of stuff to load them with," said Calieb.

"Yeah, I wonder where they are sending all the juice, then?" I pondered.

"When it gets really busy in the summer, sometimes the plant will ship directly to the customer when we get swamped. But it's only for a short time and only to specific customers. They are probably diverting some of the loads directly to the biggest customers and shorting us because they want so much one of thing," said Calieb.

"I used to remember seeing on the news strategists saying that in the event of an emergency, a hurricane or earthquake or something, most warehouses have enough for thirty days to supply the grocery stores on average. I guess this is what they mean," I said.

"Yep," said Calieb as he was called away, and other forklift operators realized that I was in the office.

We started getting pummeled with problems that we had to tackle, so that is where the end of the conversation went. I didn't look into how much product we had on hand to last us, but it wasn't like it was going to matter. The one good thing was because everything was leaving so quickly, I didn't have to worry about rotating stock because everything was spinning in and right back out so fast. So I guess that was a good thing. Hurray?

The rest of the day was pretty much the same as they day before—answering emails, helping forklift operators, blah, blah, blah—up until there was a forklift available, and then I hoped on trucks. At the end of the day, the drain was starting to eat at me.

On my way home, I had to stop for gas, so I stopped at my usual gas place, which was in Mountain Top. I had a rewards card, so I got 3¢ off a gallon when I filled up—winning! Another win was that I saw gas was down, like, 10¢. How awesome was that!

When I got home, I was beat. All I wanted to do was just lie down and take a nap. But when I pulled into the driveway, I saw the cutest thing that made me go, "You're not going to bed anytime soon, big boy." There was little Joyce, sitting on the steps with her bike helmet.

"Hi, Daddy!" she shrieked when she saw the door to my pickup truck open.

"Hi, Princess! Were you good for Mom today?" I asked as she came up and gave me a big hug.

"Yeah! Do you want to go to the park and ride bikes?"

"Sure, can we do it after dinner?" I could already smell something coming from the kitchen.

"Yeah, Mom made dinner a few minutes ago."

"Okay, good. I will take off my work boots but won't get changed, okay?"

"Okay!" she said as she and I walked into the house.

"Hey, beautiful," I said to wife Joyce as she rushed around us.

"Hey, I know you want to give me a kiss, but could it wait until after you took a shower?"

"Sure, do I smell that bad?" I asked jokingly.

Joyce had made dinner and was getting it to the table, where Clara was already sitting. She got the dinner for Peanut, me, and herself, and we all sat down to watch the news and have a little dinner. The news had on a story about how people were hoarding food and toilet paper. It was the end of the world, and the top commodity to have was toilet paper. Go figure.

"How was work today?" asked Joyce.

I kind of paused and looked down.

"What's wrong? Is everything okay?" asked Joyce in a concerned manner.

"Yeah, it's okay for right now. But I started to notice that the warehouse was getting a little empty."

"Empty? Aren't you guys always looking for space, especially right now?"

"Yeah, but we are shipping out waaay more than what we are getting in from the juice plant across the street than we normally do. I mean, we are okay for a while right now, but still," I said as I went to take a bite of dinner.

"Daddy going to run out of juice?" asked Clara.

"No, sweetie. There is going to be plenty of juice," I said reassuringly. "Do you and Mom want to come outside for a bit after we're done with dinner to go to the park and ride bikes or fly kites?"

"Yeah!" said Clara.

We cleaned up dinner and got ready to go bike riding at the park. Wife Joyce didn't want to come because she wanted a breather from the kids, so I took Joyce and Clara over to Frances Slocum with our bikes and two kites.

We found an area close to where we were on Friday but down on a lower parking lot for a change of scenery, of course. I pulled into the parking spot, and we all jumped out of the truck. Joyce helped Clara get her bike helmet on while I got our bikes out of the back of the truck. Aaand then something unbelievable happened.

As I got the last bike out of the truck and the girls were standing next to me, two large, like, passenger vans pulled up right next to me and began backing into the parking spots. There were one hundred open parking spots between any cars, and they had to park right next to me. What the hell! I noticed one plate was from Pennsylvania, but the other one was from New York. Driving the two vans were two early-thirty-something dads but not a single mom in either van. Uh-oh, that can't be good.

I heard one of the dads from the other van open his door to get out, and he said, "Okay, gang, everyone get their bikes." And just like that, about fifteen kids in each van suddenly started pouring out of every open door right next to us! *Did the governor not just shut down everything to keep the kids away from one another! What were they doing!*

It took everything I had not to scream at them because who knew what people were going to do in a pandemic? My first priority was to keep Clara and Joyce safe, so I firmly placed my hand on Peanut's shoulder, bent down, and said into her ear, "Get you and your sister back into the truck right now."

"But, Dad, there are other kids here to play with!" Joyce said disappointingly.

"Joyce, right now. Please don't argue with me. I am going to put the bikes back into the truck. You can keep your helmets on if you want. We need to leave right now."

Joyce took her little sister by the hand and went to the other side of the truck away from the vans, and they each got into their back seats. While they were doing that, I got the bikes back into the truck. I did catch one of the dads looking at me, and we locked eyes. His expression was, "Yo, bud, what's your problem? My kids not good enough to play with your kids?" The expression that I was trying to convey was "The bright side of this pandemic will mean a strong gene pool for my daughters to choose from. In the meantime, pick two of those thirty-some-odd kids you have to die and execute them now to avoid them experiencing a horrible, painfully slow death."

"Daddy, why do we have to leave all those kids?" Clara asked as we pulled away from the mass casualty event.

"Hon, it's a pandemic, okay? It means lots of people can get very sick very easily. We have to stay away from other kids and other people for a while, okay?"

"Okay, Daddy," said Clara, also disappointed that she couldn't play with the other kids. It was absolutely gut-wrenching to have to tell her that she couldn't play with other kids and seeing her reaction of being sad. She was almost all alone.

"Listen, we're going to try to find a place to go for a walk and fly kites. Would that be nice?" I asked.

"*Yes!*" Both of them excitedly yelped.

I drove to a different side of the park that had another big parking lot and a big field at the crest of a hill. This field was *perfect* for flying kites because of how the wind gently rolled over it normally almost every day. I found a spot, we got the kites, and we started to fly them.

We were about ten minutes into flying the kites. I had gotten one up into the air for Joyce and was working on the other for Clara. Clara was standing maybe fifteen yards away from me because she had seen what I had seen. A four-door silver sedan had pulled into the parking lot and, of course, parked right next to my truck. What exactly about my four-door dark-grey truck was sooo magnetic to people?

I watched the kite go up, and out of the corner of my eye, I watched Clara watching the car. An elderly couple emerged from the vehicle, and I thought, *Phew, they will know better than to come near us.* Nope.

The old man's wife then opened up the back of the car, and out popped this adorable, dark-haired little girl who was probably around three. She had on a red dress, a coat, red stockings, and play shoes; and as soon as she saw Clara at the top of the hill, she started running toward her. What happened next was heartbreaking.

"Hey, kid!" Clara yelled down to her. "You gotta stay away from us because there is a corolla virus."

The kid didn't stop, but her grandfather hopped in front of her and grabbed her hand. He looked at me, and I looked at him. He looked pissed. I maintained my composure, acknowledging that what my daughter just said to his grandkid was right. The couple started talking, and while I couldn't hear them, I imagined it wasn't anything like, "That younger man and his children are right. We need to social distance and keep the kids safe. Let's wave goodbye to the man and try to have a good time away from others." They did wave to me but not with all five fingers, just one. The older couple then got back into their car and moved to a different spot further away from us.

We were out until it got dark, at which point I told the kids that we needed to head back home. Daddy had work again tomorrow and had to go to bed early. The girls didn't put up too much of a fight and got into the truck with their kites, and we headed home.

When we got home, I put the bikes away while the kids put away their helmets and their kites. I went to find the wife and found her on the porch swing, where I joined her. Joyce and I settled back for some good old-fashioned porch swinging before we went in for the night. As we sat on the swing, we both looked at the caravan of jet planes flying thousands of feet above our heads one by one, going from west to east, carrying who-knows-what to who-knows-where. They were like airborne lifeboats abandoning a sinking ship, but where were they all going? What magical place was there that wasn't affected by this COVID-19? I looked over at Joyce, and she was just watching the show. We must have sat there for half an hour, watching it in wonder.

"Joyce, have I had a chance to tell you today that you are the most beautiful woman in the world and that I am so happy that I married you?" I said as I went to take her hand.

She pulled her hand back slowly, denying my touch, and said, "I love you too, but Arthur, can you please take a shower when you get home before you try to give me a hug and a kiss?"

She didn't have to explain to me why. I was the one being exposed now. The kids and Joyce were just home, trying to be safe. I didn't take offense to what she was asking me to do. It was a different time now.

"Okay, I know why. I don't think I should let Clara or Joyce try to hug me until I get a shower done too," I replied.

"Thank you," Joyce said softly. "I don't feel that this is something that is going to be over quickly. We are going to need to start doing stuff differently to keep Momma Joyce and myself safe."

"Like, what were you thinking about?" I asked.

"I am going to start doing groceries online for a little while. Anything we need, we can order on the grocery store's website, pick it up at the store, and then wipe it down when I get it home. We can put it in the back of your pickup truck too just to be extra safe. And the kids, I don't think it's a good idea for the kids to be around other kids right now. At school, it was really starting to get little scary. You can take them to the park, to Frances Slocum, and maybe the church parking lot, but other than that, no more shopping or anything," said Joyce.

I looked at her and said, "Yeah, I think that's a good idea. I am going to start going to the gas station up the road for gas more since they are the only station in Harding, and not a lot of out-of-towners probably go there."

"Oooh, good thinking. I didn't think about that. I talked to my mom today. She is going to cancel all of her doctor's visits for the next few months. Speaking of that, how is your thing doing?" She pointed at my crotch.

"Actually, it has been really sore lately," I said.

"I bet you probably went back to work too soon," said Joyce as she got up to go back in the house.

I decided to follow her. "Yeah, I probably did. But they needed me back at work, and that was *before* there was a pandemic. Hey, Joyce, remember when you said it wasn't going to be the end of the world if I got a vasectomy? National tragedy."

"Oh, shut up! Come on, let's get the kids and everyone in bed."

Chapter 8

Day 8

March 16, 2020, Monday

Beep, beep, beep.

That blasted sleep-stealing machine! Boy, did I hate that alarm clock. I rolled over to give Joyce a quick kiss on her exposed…shoulder? I don't know anymore. Everything was just starting to blur together anyway. I got myself ready for work, went out the door, and wondered, *What is it going to be today?*

On the drive in, I didn't turn on the radio again. It was a weird feeling. Part of me was very, very, very grateful to still be working and have my job. But at the same time, I was very, like, worried. What would happen if I had it but didn't show symptoms and brought it home to Joyce and the kids? But another part of me was pretty much driving through it. I had to push through it. If I didn't go to work and everyone else stopped going to work, the food supply infrastructure actually *would* fall apart, and then we'd have food insecurity and then pretty much societal collapse as we knew it.

I clocked in, walked to the office, and started to work. I was there for a while when Big Boss walked by.

"Good morning, Art," he said as he came into the office.

I got my information for the week's key performance indicators and went to Big Boss's office to do what I had to do there with him.

"KPI stuff?" he asked.

"Yep. Hey, just so you know, with what the president said on Friday and everything, my family told me to come into work unless martial law is declared or Joyce doesn't feel it's safe for me to go in," I said, trying to reassure him that I would be there to support the operations.

"Good, we're going to need everyone here. Tell everyone mandated ten-hour days still. I don't know what this weekend is going to be like," he said as I got up.

"Gotcha," I said as I prepared to start the shift.

Just then, Jim came in with the notes for the preshift meeting. "Here you guys go," he said as he put it down on Big Boss's desk.

I started going over everything—lots of inbounds, lots of outbounds, blah, blah, blah. So nothing new there, but at the corner of the bottom of the page, a little note caught my eye.

"Hey, Big Boss," I said as I started to read what the note said. "What is this message? *Effective immediately, no outside food deliveries allowed until further notice. This includes but is not limited to...*" It started to list off all the places that weren't allowed to deliver food.

"What do you care? You never order lunch. Joyce won't let you," said Big Boss.

"Excuse me? I do whatever I want whenever I want. I don't need her permission to get lunch!" I said, trying to sound like I was in control.

"Uh-huh. Hey, who here in the office is friends with Arthur on social media?" asked Big Boss.

Several hands went up.

"So who wants to be the first one to say something to Joyce?" asked Big Boss smiling.

"Please don't. Anyway, what is that message for?" I asked.

"Corporate doesn't want any outside food vendors bringing the virus into the building. So no more deliveries until we are told that it is okay to do so. Until then, everyone must bring in their lunch from home in a sealed plastic bag," said Big Boss.

"Didn't affect anyone on my shift," said Jim.

"Well, that's easy. There isn't anything open on your shift" I replied. "Big Boss, can you come out with me this morning to tell everyone? They are just going to bum-rush your office anyway. You might as well get out in front of it before they trample themselves trying to get in here."

Big Boss nodded in agreement, and before long, we were both outside, announcing to everyone the new, impromptu policy. Most of the guys just stood around, looked at the ground, and nodded. There were a few that said that they didn't know about the policy change and that they didn't bring in their lunch and asked what we were going to do for them. I agreed with them. How were they supposed to know what was going on when no one told them! Couldn't someone have called over the weekend when they were making the policy change? I don't know. I do know that Big Boss agreed with them, and for just today, as long as the deliveries were left at the guard shack instead of brought to the building, then it was okay. The forklift operators then could just go to the guard shack to get their food—just for today, though.

The rest of the day was just busy. But for me, the big thing about today wasn't what was going on at work; tonight was the township supervisors' work session meeting. While it was open to the public, generally, no one really went to them because there was no input allowed from the audience. I had been asked a while ago to come to this one because a representative from PennDOT, the Pennsylvania Department of Transportation, was supposed to be there to discuss any road problems anyone was having. In Harding, I have been known to be quite "vocal" about problems, so a few of the supervisors figured I could give them some actual substance.

When I finally did clock out and start to head home, the first thing that I began to notice was the traffic. Or lack of any of it. There wasn't any traffic! It was like a holiday. There were no school buses or long lines at the traffic light before I got to the interstate. Then when I was on the interstate, it was like I was one of maybe fifteen people heading north. This was going to be different for sure!

Because there was no school and everyone was home, I drove up to Momma Joyce's house first and took care of her coal stove. After that, when I pulled into the driveway, the first thing I noticed was that there was something zip-tied to the deck. I got out of my truck and walked toward the house, and on the railing going up the stairs was a bottle of hand sanitizer zip-tied to a post. I just stared at it.

"Sanitize your hands, mister!" yelled someone from way above me.

I looked up and saw Joyce hanging out of a window that was upstairs.

"Hon?" I asked quizzically, pointing at the bottle of hand sanitizer.

"I had an extra bottle, so I left one outside for you to use before you come into the house," she hollered back.

As I stood there, slowly pumping the sanitizer into my hands, reflecting and pondering the new reality I was living in, Clara popped out of the front door, yelling, "Daddy!" as she came running toward me, hands out stretched to open the gate and give me a hug.

"Clara, stop!" I yelled.

She did as I had asked her to, but she stood there, looking like I was angry at her. She looked confused, scared, and hurt that I just screamed at her for something she had no idea was wrong. Now I felt bad.

"Hon," I said as I got down on my knee and looked at her through the gate, "Daddy just got home from work, and because of COVID-19 and Daddy being out, I don't want you to give me a hug until I take a shower, okay, sweetie? You're not in trouble or anything. You didn't do anything wrong. I love you very much. You're my little princess, right?"

"Right, I'm your little princess!" She cheered right up.

"And I want to keep my little princess safe! Thank you, sweetie," I said as I stood up again. I looked up at the window and at Joyce, who had witnessed the whole thing. She looked like she was about to cry now. I blew her a kiss. She smiled a bit and blew one back, but I couldn't let them know how much this was killing me too right now. Daddy had to be strong for everyone right now. Besides, men weren't allowed to cry.

"Hon, do you need anything before I go take a shower?" I yelled up to the window.

"No, come on up here. I will get you some clothes so you don't have to touch anything and then get dinner started!" she yelled back.

"Hey, are you still okay with me going to the township supervisors' work session tonight to talk to the PennDOT guy?" I asked before I stepped into the house.

"Yes, but try to keep your distance from everyone," she said as she closed the window.

Clara opened all the doors for me so I could get into the house. I got in and went upstairs to take my shower. After my shower, I opened up the bathroom door, and standing there was Clara, waiting for me to give her a hug.

"Sweetie, were you waiting here the entire time?" I asked.

"Yeah, Dad. You still need to give me my hug!" she said as she lunged at my legs with her little hands.

I leaned down and gave her a big hug back.

We went downstairs, and as Joyce was busy making dinner, I went and worked on the coal fire with Clara in tow. Lord knew where my oldest one was—probably sitting in her bed, playing on her tablet. Clara was fun to have for the time being because she wanted to see inside the coal furnace all the while asking, "Why is coal dirty, Dad? How does coal burn, Dad? Why does it smell so bad when it burns, Dad?" Jeepers cripes almighty, kiddo, you sure did have a lot of questions. Say what you would, but Joyce and I didn't think you could beat coal heat—not baseboard heaters, not propane, and certainly not heating oil if you want to talk about smell. Oh dear!

"How was your day?" asked Joyce as we all sat down to dinner. Somehow we found Peanut, and she was sitting at the table, already waiting.

"A living nightmare. Everyone is hoarding so much. It's hard to keep up. We are short-staffed and have waaay more trucks than we normally have. Heard anything from the school?" I asked as I sat down.

"No, not yet. If we are going to be out for a while, I have some educational books and stuff here that we can use for Peanut until they figure out what they are going to do," said Joyce.

I looked at both the girls and asked, "Were you guys good for Mommy today?"

"Yea," replied Joyce.

"What did you guys do today?"

"We played dolls!" said Clara.

"Any word on how much longer you guys are going to be mandated overtime?" asked Joyce.

"Boss said this morning that there will be mandated overtime for ten hours all this week. He doesn't know about the weekend. I would not count on me being home this weekend," I said as I ate.

Joyce nodded her head silently.

"Are you okay? I know it's a lot of overtime," I asked, trying to see how she was feeling.

"I will manage. I am not angry at you because this entire thing is totally out of your control."

That made me feel slightly better. Everyone continued eating dinner, and I put away all the dishes. The kids went upstairs to play, and I had a few minutes to watch the news and pet Buster before I had to leave for the meeting.

"The supervisors are still going to have their meeting today?" asked Joyce as we watched the news and I petted the dog on the floor.

"I sent a message to one supervisor, and they said yes. The supervisors' meeting is still going to be held because they're essential government workers."

"What time is the meeting?" asked Joyce.

I looked up at the clock in the living room and realized I had about ten minutes to get there.

"I better head out now, actually. Mind if I get my kiss?" I asked as I got up off the floor and over to Joyce's chair. I leaned in, and she gave me a quick kiss, which was reassuring, to say the least, given everything that was going on.

"Be safe and stay away from people at the meeting," she said as I started to go out the door.

"You got it, boss lady."

I headed down to the Exeter Township Municipal Building, where I saw basically just the supervisors' cars in the parking lot.

See, we said we lived in Harding, which was true. But Harding was a village within the township of Exeter in Luzerne County. We had no post office, police department, or elected officials, but our fire trucks and ambulances said it. I won't bore you with the details but the reason one would say they're from Harding was because there were three Exeters right next to each other. There was Exeter Township— Wyoming County right above us; Exeter Township—Luzerne County, which was us; and Exeter Borough, which was below us. Because Exeter Borough was more populated, if you said you were from Exeter, everyone would assume you meant the borough. If you were in Exeter Township—Wyoming County, it was generally known you were from the Falls area. I won't bore you with the details on why this was like this, but it is. In fact, there are three Exeter Townships in the state of Pennsylvania that I knew about.

Aaanyway, I pulled into the parking lot and walked into the building. The township building had two levels: the top floor with the general meeting area, a kitchen off to the left, and bathrooms and the supervisors'/secretary's offices off to the right. I went into the supervisors' office just in time to see that they were about to start the meeting with the pledge of allegiance. It was the supervisors, the chief of police, and me. I stood off to the side and said the pledge with them. I did not intend to speak at the meeting the entire time since I was there as a guest to talk to PennDOT, not to gossip with the supervisors.

"Hey, Mr. Becker," said one of the supervisors. "Nice to see you."

"Hi, everyone. I know that you had asked me to be here, so I will stay quietly off to the side." I replied.

"Art Becker, quiet? That's a laugh!" said another supervisor. "No, it's fine, Artie. Take a seat. It's gonna be a while."

"Why?" I asked.

"I'll explain why. Let's start the meeting, shall we?" said the chairman of the board of supervisors.

See, we didn't have a mayor; we had a board of supervisors that was led by a chairman, and there was a vice chairman to fill in when the chairman wasn't there. "PennDOT is not sending their representative today. Nor will they be sending anyone for the foreseeable future."

"What? Why?" asked one of the supervisors.

"The state is in a declared state of emergency. They are stopping everything as of right now, so no new PennDOT projects in the township for a while," replied the chairman. "Just so everyone is aware, the township of Exeter Luzerne County is in a state of emergency as well as every other township in the state of Pennsylvania."

That caught me very off guard. The township was in a state of emergency? How? Why? When were they going to tell everyone, or was this something that was just generally known? Maybe I didn't quite understand what that meant, or maybe I was misinterpreting something.

"That's because, folks, the township will now have access to any financial or other resources that the state can provide to help the fire, EMS, and police departments pay for things like PPE, equipment, etc.," said the vice chairman.

"Yes, the town's two fire departments and the Harding Mt Zion Ambulance company are going to be getting extra PPE and getting training and procedures ready on how to handle calls and casualties," said one of the other supervisors.

When he said the word *casualties*, I thought everyone in the room paused as we all kind of took in the seriousness of the situation. Our mostly volunteer force was now going to be exposed to a potentially deadly virus as they start hauling "casualties" out of houses. *How many people are going to volunteer for that?* I wondered.

"I think this situation is going to get a lot worse before it gets better," said one of the supervisors.

"We're going to need to follow the guidance from the state and monitor anything in the township. Everyone needs to just keep calm and not let people think we are nervous because we cannot have a panic in town," said the chairman.

After reviewing the emergency, the supervisors went on to the normal business for the township. When the chairman dismissed the meeting, I rushed over really quick to try to get a hold of the chief of police.

"Hey, Chief," I said, trying to flag him down.

"Hey, Artie. What's up?" said Chief.

"Hey, how are you doing?" I asked, trying to casually start a quick conversation.

"I'm okay, all things considered. Yourself? How are Joyce and the kids?" he asked.

"We're okay, but I have a question. It's about Joyce and the kids. I wanted to ask you something," I said.

"Sure, what's up?" he said.

"Hey, so where I work, at the juice company, we're getting mandated overtime every day and on weekends. I am not home nearly as much as I want to be, considering what's going on. I wanted to know if, when your officers have downtime, you know, no calls or anything pressing, if they would take a quick drive by my house to check on the girls. Not saying that I think anything is going to happen, but the world, as crazy as it is right now, I don't know. I want Joyce to know it's okay and safe," I said nervously.

The chief looked down for a second and then looked at me. "I know what you're saying. I don't think any of my officers would have a problem with that." He could see the relieved look on my face.

"Thank you sooo much, Chief. I really appreciate that."

Chief smiled and said, "No problem. You have a good night and look over that family."

"I will," I said as I walked out of the township building.

When I got home, I could see that Joyce was outside on the porch swing through the window. As I was walking through the kitchen on my way to out to her, on the table, I saw the homework that her and Peanut were going over. As I picked up the papers, I saw at the bottom of the pile a blue loose-leaf paper notebook. My curiosity got to me. *Maybe these are some drawings that Peanut was doing,* I thought. I picked it up, and on the first page, I saw some notes in my wife's handwriting. With notebook in hand, I headed outside to read further and talk with Joyce.

I went over to join my wife and sat down. She was quiet, looking up into the sky. I was wondering what she was staring at or thinking about, but then I could see it too. It the night sky, against the backdrop of the stars behind them, was the seemingly unending line of airplanes with their strobe lights blinking. It was like a conveyor belt of blinking lights moving among the stars.

"How was the meeting?" asked Joyce.

I told her everything that was said except for the part about the police patrolling by the house more often. I didn't think she would mind that I asked them to do it, but I didn't want her to think that I thought she was weak or anything. She was the strongest woman I knew, of course, but still, I didn't want her to think I was a jerk for asking the police to do that.

As I talked about what happened, she sat quietly until I was finished.

"So the town is in a state of emergency, eh?" she asked.

"Yep," I said.

"And it doesn't look like anyone knows what the virus is or what it can do?"

"Yep."

As we were sitting there, she tapped on the notebook with her fingers.

"I wanted to show you this," she said as she took the notebook from me. "I've started to keep a journal about everything that is happening."

I took it from her. "Wow, is this something you started for the kids? Something to look back on years from now when this is all over?"

"For the kids, for our grandkids, for whoever. I think that something like this is one of the most important things we have ever been through in our lives," she said.

As I looked through it, I said, "If I ever write a book about what is happening to us during this, do you mind if I use some of your notes?"

Joyce looked at me and smiled. "Sure, are you ever really, *really*, ever going to write a book about all this?"

I kind of paused and said, "I don't know. Maybe. Have I had a chance to tell you today that I think that you are the most beautiful woman in the world and that I am so happy that I married you?"

"I love you too," replied Joyce.

Joyce's Journal

Days leading up…
COVID-19
- coronavirus diseases, Wuhan, China, 2019
- primarily spread between people via respiratory droplets from coughs and sneezes

Friday, March 13, 2020

Afternoon—Local superintendents from schools decided a minimum of 5 days school closed. Almost an hour later, PA governor Wolf closes all public schools for a minimum of 10 business days (2 weeks). In the days before, hand sanitizer was difficult to find. I purchased several weeks ahead.

I continued to use my own Lysol in my classroom. Students were beginning to ask to fill their little hand sanitizer bottles from my bottle. My curriculum was to watch a musical, which I felt would let kids' minds wander from what was happening around the world. That afternoon, I gathered my coat, lunch box, and yes, my own Lysol. And I shut down and unplugged all technology, knowing schools would be shut down.

I had never experienced anything like this. What will become of this missed time? Keep kids safe. Keep all kids and families safe. Keep my family safe. Arthur and I took kids bike riding and flew kites. Social distancing.

Saturday March 14, 2020

Staying home—Very blessed to be able to stay home. My mother taught me to always have extra. I bought some extra Tylenol and Motrin about 3 weeks ago for both kids and adults. I bought soap, disinfectant, and hand sanitizer a few weeks ago also.

My husband, Arthur Becker, is now working 7 days a week. Water in bottles is in high demand, and so is juice. We no longer go to grocery store and likely will not for some time. We order some things online. Girls and I did yard work and played outside.

Sunday March 15, 2020

Social distancing. Nice to live in a rural area. Had breakfast/lunch then went outside for a bit. Husband came home from work and took kids to ride bikes and fly kites. He told me they geared up, and then a whole bunch of other kids piled out of big SUVs, so he took girls for a walk. SOCIAL DISTANCING.

Husband and I sat on porch swing and raised a glass to everyone who drove by. Watched president and vice president talk about how great things are going. Fed reserve slashed rates to almost 0%.

First case of COVID-19 in Luzerne County. Many buildings and county municipal buildings limiting access.

CDC beginning to make recommendations that no one should gather in groups of 25+ for at least 8 weeks (2 months).

My husband asks me what I think. My response is now…I don't know because people are crowding stores for toilet paper, etc. People are unpredictable. I am taking it seriously because my mom, Joyce, is 79 and on oxygen 24/7. I worry for her the most. Supermarkets that were 24/7 are now closing overnight to restock. Still not going.

How difficult to tell your children to enjoy this last banana because we won't have them all the time. I did ask Arthur to go to the Farmstand to get apples so that we could have fresh fruit.

Monday March 16, 2020

Breakfast and then some work sheets for our 3rd grader and computer education games for the 5 year old. Adverbs—how, when, where.

Played badminton for outside activity. Husband got apples and pears from local orchard store.

Down—Stock market down almost 3 thousand points. NY Governor questions national choices during this time. Curfews for gyms, restaurants, etc. @ 8 p.m. in NY State. PA followed suit this evening. Hospitals are beginning to cancel elective surgeries. PA gov. announced wine and spirits (PLCB) will close indefinitely tomorrow @ 9 p.m.

Chapter 9

Day 9: Fly-over Days

March 17, 2020, Tuesday

Beep, beep, beep.

I went to slap the stupid alarm clock silent but swung three times before I finally hit the thing. I leaned over to face Joyce, and in the very dim light of the room, she remained to be the most beautiful woman I had ever seen. I leaned in and gave her a kiss on her forehead. "I love you," I whispered to her. Before I had a chance to lean back and leave, her arm wrapped itself around my neck, and she patted me on the back.

"I love you too."

Boy, that was nice.

I did my normal morning routine: I headed downstairs, got my coffee and lunch ready, nearly tripped over the dogs as I walked out the door, and headed off to work. I turned on the morning talk radio station and listened to the news today. Going to work this time was much different than it normally was. The way I normally went into work was I'd take the back roads from Harding down into what was called locally as the valley. The valley is a general term for all the cities and towns that are in the Wyoming Valley of Pennsylvania, the northernmost point being Carbondale and the southernmost point being the Wilkes-Barre/Nanticoke area.

Anyway, the normal way into work was through the backroads from Harding into the valley and then up the mountain to Mountain

Top. It saved me about fourteen miles in my round trip on my vehicle and gas. But COVID-19…COVID-19 has changed the way I thought about that stuff now. Did I want to risk breaking down or getting stuck in the little cities and towns between me and work, or did I want take the expressways to work, which, while longer in miles, was faster? I Better not risk it, so I was going to take the expressways.

The expressway was the Cross Valley Expressway or PA 309. It stretched across the lower/midsection of the valley. It was closer to Wilkes-Barre than it was to Scranton, which was fine with me. I didn't like going to Lackawanna County anyway. To get to the expressway, I followed the back roads to where it began and then followed it to Interstate 81. This was depressing. Fourteen extra miles to travel, and for what? What were the chances that I got stuck in one of these cities, and what were the chances I'd encounter someone who was sick? Was it the same as breaking down on the expressway? *Ugh, what do I do?*

I forged my way onto the highway, and I didn't have to travel too far to notice something, well, off. Distance aside, I didn't generally like to travel the highways because there was so much traffic! I would either be waiting in it or just trying to dodge other cars on it. PA 309 and I-81 were major highways in this area, and they were constantly filled with cars. But today, it was not a holiday or a weekend; today it was literally just me on the road and a handful of tractor trailers and delivery trucks. I knew I didn't miss a memo or something. I guessed people were actually paying attention to the lockdown orders.

Work was the same as it had been since last week—exhaustingly busy. I was very, very, very thankful still that I had a job and, where everyone else was being cut hours or flat-out laid off, I was getting overtime. However, the workload had no end in sight, and there were very few additional resources—except for one guy.

Wisecracker, who was on the weekend shift, volunteered to come extra hours. While we were all mandated, the weekend shift was sort of absolved on account that we simply didn't have enough forklifts to accommodate everyone. And of course, during the day, this happened.

"Yo, Artie," said Wisecracker as he pulled up on his forklift, which just happened to be the oldest one in the fleet and that no one used, not even me unless I absolutely had to. "I have to use this one?"

"Are there any other ones left for you to use?" I asked.

"No, just this old POS," he replied.

"Then I don't know what to tell you, playa. You've got to take that one. Besides, an experienced professional like yourself should have no issues doing what you need to do with that equipment," I said with a snarky attitude.

"You know why no one likes this forklift, dude? It's like you. Has no balls!" he said as he tried speed away at literally like four miles an hour.

I just kind of shook my head as Kurt, who apparently saw the whole thing, came up from behind me.

"Don't you pay no attention to that guy, Mr. Art. you are doing a heck of a job today. Did anyone tell you that?" said Kurt.

"You know what? No, you're the first one. And you're doing a heck of a job too, bud," I replied.

"How is the weekend looking?" he asked.

I pointed to the warehouse and said, "About as good as the warehouse."

We both looked around and saw that it was ever so slowly getting more and more empty each day.

"Boy, we're going to run out of stuff soon," said Kurt.

"Yeah, I know. We're shipping more out than we are getting in. This is going to get interesting in a few more weeks," I said.

We then went back to going about our day. I kept on resolving issues and trying to do my job. Finally, when the time to punch out came, I saw Mark.

"Artemus," said Mark as I waited by the time clock.

"Marky-Mark, how are you?" I asked.

"Is this going to end?" asked Mark.

"Ha, yeah, at some point. Just hope there is someone around to process my life insurance policy for my family when it does," I said, and we both laughed.

"It's crazy! Last night we had so many drivers that there were almost fistfights out in the parking lot," said Mark. "Anything I need to know right off the bat?"

"Got one or two returns in the stage. All the missing pallets have been reported. Freshness is okay. Other than that, not really," I said. "Notice how empty it is starting to get around here?"

"Yeah, in the cooler, it's getting pretty empty. I saw it when I was doing my cycle counts," said Mark.

"Well, on the bright side, counting the warehouse is going to get pretty easy when it's empty," I said.

We both kind of laughed again.

"All right, see you tomorrow. I left you a new battery in the forklift," I said as I went to punch out for the day.

"You the man! Later, Artemus."

I left to go home that day and once again took notice of the light traffic. Getting home was going to be easier or at least less dangerous with no one on the road to hit me! I wondered when gas was going to start to go down.

After I got home and finished working on both coal stoves, I was finally able to step foot in the door after I washed my hands with sanitizer, which was on the porch, of course. Then after, I told the kids that they couldn't hug Daddy until after he decontaminated in the shower…of course. Man, this whole "new normal" thing blew.

At the end of the evening, after all the hustle and shuffle of playing with the kids or doing whatever, Joyce and I sat on the porch swing. We drank our adult beverages and raised them to each car going by, a "*Heeeyyy!*" coming out of each of our screaming mouths in an effort to raise the spirits of our neighbors, who were probably going through the same thing we were. As we tried to make the most of the situation, every now and then, we would take a look up in the sky at the seemingly endless convoy of airplanes making their way above us.

"Joyce, have I had a chance to tell you today that I think you are the most beautiful woman in the world and that I am so happy that I married you?" I asked, swinging with her.

"I love you too. I am going to try to put an online order at the grocery store next week. Do you need anything?" she asked.

"Not that I can think of off the top of my head. Do you want to go alone, or do you want me and the kids to come with you?" I asked, knowing full well that she probably won't want anyone to go with her.

"No, just let me have your pickup truck. I will use that. They can put the groceries in the back, and I will clean them off when I get home. I am going to try to make it later in the day, so I will take it when you get home," said Joyce.

"Gotcha, boss lady."

Joyce's Journal

Tuesday, March 17, 2020

Breakfast—NY Gov closed NY schools. Their 180 day requirement will be waved 2 weeks for now.

Final day for purchase of liquor at wine & spirits shops.

Hospitals in area begin to set up tents outside ERs in response. They want to be ready to activate, treat, and release from the tents. 3 cases reported (discharge) at hospital in Danville.

Very grateful my mother taught me some of her weird ways. We used bubble gloves, and we will do little snapits tomorrow. She always had neat things around her house. So glad that I do that too...

Happy St. Patrick's Day!

Day 10

March 18, 2020, Wednesday

I am up. I am up? What the hell, man? Why am I up before the alarm clock? I hope that damned thing doesn't—

Beep, beep, beep.

I leaned over to give Joyce a kiss on her forehead. "I love you," I whispered to her before I left. She rolled over to her other side, snoring—a signal to me that it was time to go.

The ride into work was just as eerie as the day before, with only me and scattered amounts of tractor trailers on the highway. As I traveled over the bridges and could see down on the streets below, not a soul was to be seen. I noticed this morning that I could still see a line of airplanes in the sky, going east, all marching dutifully to a destination that only they knew. In the meantime, I'd better get to where I knew I had to go.

The office was busy, the warehouse floor was essentially borderline organized chaos, and everyone was stressed. I would make jokes here and there to try to lift their spirits in the hopes that it would help. Sometimes they did, but right now, everyone had basically one thing left on their minds.

"Artie," said Big Boss with a sigh as I walked into the office from the warehouse for a reason that escaped me at the moment I was writing this, "let everyone know that we are going to be mandated this weekend."

"Yeah, I figured. Both days?" I asked.

"Yeah, both days. Is there a chance you could work more hours?" he asked.

I thought about it. Right now I was working ten hours, so what was another hour?

"Even if there isn't a forklift?" I asked.

"At this point, anyone who can come in and help is needed. Can you work more hours?" he asked again.

"Yeah, want me to adjust my schedule?" I asked.

"Anything you can do, yes. Better let Joyce know," he said as he walked into his office.

"I will send her a text message," I replied as I turned on the mobile data on my phone. Before I had a chance to let her know, I got a message from her asking if I was still going to be required to go to work if they shut down interstate commerce.

I was so exhausted emotionally and physically that I just blurted out into the room, "Hey, boss, Joyce wants to know if we are still going to be required to come in to work if they shut down interstate commerce," and as the words left my mouth, it was like the whole room became stunned. You could have heard a pin drop as everyone didn't stare at me. They just stared out into space as the bleak, very real possibility that the government may shut down interstate commerce started to set in.

"Well, let me go ask," said Big Boss. I went back to my phone and sat at my desk, patiently waiting for an answer from Big Boss and answering my emails. It didn't take long for an answer, and instead of yelling it from his office into the room, he called my desk phone.

"Hey, I didn't want to yell this into the office. I called the director of transportation. According to transportation, if they shut down interstate commerce, we're still going to be open because they're going to let our trucks go through. Any trucks with food, fuel, medical supplies, automotive supplies, and construction stuff will be allowed to cross," said Big Boss.

I am not saying that he took the wind out of my sails, but man, a weekend or two off would be sweet. "Okay, thanks. I will let Joyce know," I replied as I began to text Joyce that I had been asked to work the weekend again and longer hours. I also asked her if she was going to be okay with everything or if she wanted me to resist the mandated overtime and come home to her and the kids on top of telling her that there was no closure for us in the event they shut down the state borders.

I continued on with my day. I finished my work, saw Mark, and left. The drive home was met with less traffic than the day before. I guessed it wasn't all bad news.

I took care of the coal stoves at both houses and went into the house after rubbing down my arms and hands with hand sanitizer, and waiting for me at the kitchen table was Peanut. She had two badminton rackets, a couple of birdies, and a smile.

"Hi, Daddy!" said Joyce, all bright-eyed and bushy-tailed.

"Hey, Joyce. Do you want to play badminton with Daddy?" I asked.

"Yes! Can we pleassse!" she asked.

No matter how much I was hurting that day, no matter how tired I was, I just couldn't say no to that little girl. "All right, hon. Let Daddy take off his steel-toed boots, okay?"

She darted out of the room and came back with my sneakers before I even had a chance to get them myself. I took off my boots as wife Joyce and Clara came into the room. We all headed out to the lawn to play. Peanut grabbed the stick that we used to separate the zones, and we began. She was slowly getting better at this game. At one point, wife Joyce jumped in and played with Peanut against me while Clara rolled around in the grass.

After the game, Joyce and I once again took our spots on the porch swing. The kids, well, they went running into the house to play video games. We rocked back and forth on the chair and were going,

"*Heeeyyy!*" to any passing cars again. Some waved, others honked, and some didn't even see us.

"Hey, Joyce, have I had a chance to tell you that I think you're the most beautiful woman in the world and that I love you?" I asked.

"I love you too. Did you happen to look up?" she replied with her hand outstretched and pointing toward the sky.

We both looked up and saw…a lot of nothing. It was a good while before we finally saw an airplane flying above us—just one single, lonely airplane flying across the sky. It was like someone switched off a light. The endless line of airplanes was over, and now, well, now who knew what that one single plane, which we waited ten minutes to see, was doing? Where did it come from? Where was it going? What were the people on the plane thinking about?

"I guess that wherever everyone was getting to, they got to," I said. "Did you try to put that order in at the grocery store? Again, I will get milk, eggs, butter, and bread from the gas station when I stop, so don't worry about that kind of stuff."

"No, we still have plenty of food for a good while. I will hold off until I absolutely have to. Just don't stop anywhere like you have been doing. Just come home right from work. Come on, let's go inside. I will make dinner," said Joyce.

Joyce's Journal

Wednesday, March 18, 2020

Breakfast—Worksheets for Joyce.
Plan to put up Easter decorations today.
Husband's work is asking him to work more
hours. I hope he stays safe.
President has activated the US ships Mercy
and Comfort. They are medical/hospital ships.
One will be in NY harbor, the other at San Diego.
A Georgia hospital is sewing mask covers
out of vinyl to extend the life span of their N95

masks. Hospitals, some, have used a 6-month supply of masks, protective wear in 5–7 days.

Stock market down around 2,000 points.

Sports have been postponed or cancelled.

The girls' dance studio shut down a few days ago.

Day 11

March 19, 2020, Thursday

Beep, beep, beep.

I slapped the stupid alarm clock silent. I leaned over to face Joyce and gave her a kiss on her forehead. "I love you," I whispered to her before I left. Only one more day until—awww, who was I kidding? This wasn't going to end anytime soon.

I got myself ready to go to work quickly, and out the door I went. I nearly tripped over Buster, who was lying on the floor of the mudroom next to Shaggy.

"Take it easy, guys. I'll see you later," I muttered half groggily as I went out into the darkness toward my truck. Buster basically picked his head up and cocked it to one side to quizzically stare at me, then back to the sleep he went.

The ride in was getting tooo eerie. This morning, there wasn't even any truck traffic. I was literally the only car on the freeway. The *one* good thing was that we seemed to have plateaued with our volume of trucks waiting to get to the building. The line was *not* longer than it was the day before. Granted, it was still *extremely* long, just not longer.

I was at my desk with all the commotion going on in the office when Big Boss called me on my office phone.

"Art, you busy?"

I just laughed. "Of course not, Boss. I am just kind of twiddling my thumbs here at the moment."

"Okay, good. Listen, I have good news, and I have bad news for you."

"Oh, what the heck? Give me the bad news," I said.

"We are going to be getting a lot of returns coming at us quick," said Big Boss.

Oh, wow, now? We were in the middle of a pandemic—a national emergency, and someone wanted to actually *return* product to us? Who on earth was… You know what? Whatever.

"Seriously? Who?" I exclaimed.

"Not that it even matters, but you only need one guess to figure out who it is. Just know that they are coming back," replied Boss.

"Oh no." I just kind of sagged my head. This customer was one of our largest, probably our biggest, customer by volume. If they were sending back returns right now, there was probably a good reason. "How many?"

"Right now they are sending these emails load by load, but I don't know. Twenty or thirty."

"*Twenty or thirty returns, full truckloads?*" I nearly fell over in my seat.

"Yes, full truckloads. And don't bother asking me why. The reason they are returning them is because of miscellaneous reasons on the emails." He cut me off before I even had a chance to ask.

"So we literally have hundreds of trucks that we need to either load or unload right now, and we are going to toss on twenty or thirty more. No one besides Mark and me have the training to do them, so it is literally going to be on just us. We don't have the space on the docks to do our normal auditing of a return. We're going to have to audit the product still in the trailer…" I tried to keep going.

"Art, stop. This is going to happen. Get it done, and no, you can't have any help. We have waaay too little manpower to handle what we are doing right now."

Wow, he was good.

I just sort of threw my hands up in the air. He was right; there was nothing we could do to get out of it. I had to work on them now.

On the bright side, that many returns would benefit us because our volume in the warehouse was getting lower, so it would be helpful to have that many inbounds to use for other trucks.

"Do we have an ETA on any of these?" I asked.

"No, but given where they are all coming from, and they still need to get carriers scheduled to bring them back, I would say sometime Monday next week, they should start coming in," he said.

"Ugh, all right, you're right, boss. What is the good news then?" I asked.

Click.

The phone hung up.

"Well," I said, disparagingly staring out into space, "that isn't too optimistic."

I get it. We were the warehouse, and this was what we did. It was what we were paid for and what we were trained for. There were other warehouses with five times the volume and work that we had. On the flip side, those other warehouses were five times bigger with five times the staff. This was all just so overwhelming sometimes, but we couldn't let it shut us down. We must just carry on the best we could.

I finished off the day working with Mark on some problems because since I was staying later, I was crossing over with Mark onto some of his shift. It was nice to get out of there at quitting time, and even though—*even though*—we were mandated to work that weekend, it was still nice knowing that tomorrow was going to be Friday.

I got home and did my normal route. The only thing different I did today was I brought up Momma Joyce's mail with me. It was starting to collect in her mailbox, and I didn't want the mail lady to think she was dead or anything. Other than that, it was just the normal work on the fireplaces, telling the kids not to hug Dad until I took a shower, taking a shower, and then playing with the kids while Joyce worked on something for dinner.

After dinner, the kids went upstairs, and Joyce and I went out on the porch swing. We held up our adult beverages to all the passing cars, noticed again that there was no airplane traffic in the sky *at all*, and chatted. Then I noticed something a bit different at the neighbor's house. As we rocked back and forth, I nudged Joyce in the arm and said, "What do you think is going on over there?"

Our neighbors were a couple a little older than us, but they had grandkids. They were in their driveway, hugging each other while the wife was waving into a car window that they were standing in front of. We were way too far away from each other to see their faces, which, of course, that's how it was in Harding, but I could kind of make out a distinct faint conversation. It was like they were yelling at someone who was in the car.

Joyce sighed. "Their kids bring over the new grandbaby in the car. They are afraid of giving the baby anything, but they are so desperate to see them. So they stand outside and try to talk with the baby." She could see that I instantly slumped in my spot on the chair. "It has been going on a for a few days now, but it happens either when you are at work or when you have gone to sleep. They can't even hold the baby. Can you imagine?"

"Yeah, I can imagine. Hell, right now, I have to tell the kids not to hug Daddy until I get a shower and decontaminate. It's what we have to do right now, hon. If they are sick and don't know it, they'll get the baby sick. If the baby has it and no one knows it, then the baby gets them sick," I said.

"Yeah, you're right," she said as we quietly watched what was going on.

When the neighbors were done talking with the baby, the car pulled away. Both of them smiled and waved, but when the car was out of sight, they collapsed into each other. And while we couldn't hear them, their body language told us that there was a little sobbing going on. I couldn't run over and tell them, but it wasn't just them that were sobbing. Right now it felt like it was the whole world.

"You have that gas mask in your truck still, right?" asked Joyce.

I was looking at the ground as we gently swung. After she asked that, I slowly I looked up at her and nodded my head. "Yeah, it's somewhere in my truck. Why?"

"If you ever feel that there is something going on or something wrong at work, promise me you will use it," she said.

"Okay. Hey, Joyce," I said as I grabbed her hand, "have I had a chance to tell you today that I think that you are the most beautiful woman in the world and that I am so happy that I married you?"

"I love you too," said Joyce.

Joyce's Journal

Thursday March 19, 2020

Breakfast—News is reporting home health-care workers are making their own protective gear. Where is all this stuff? CDC allowing health-care workers who have been exposed to virus to keep working.

Government is to send out some stimulus check by April 5th up to $1,000 depending on income levels.

NY gov asking businesses to cut workforce to 25%.

President Conference—2 medical ships and suggesting using Carnival Cruise Lines as hospitals. What? President lets reporters know they are sitting to close and should just let 2 or 3 that he likes be at the press briefings. What? This isn't time for his jokes, etc.?

My work is asking us to share websites as resources. Kids and parents aren't going to use them. I will share a few but leave families be. We have many kids that I am sure are only on social media/video games. For what? I added a few to our department's online docs.

PA gov. has closed all nonessential businesses. I got paid today. We aren't sure how this will work with our retirement plans yet. Will this time off be seen as nonwork toward retirement? We have been reassured that we will still be paid.

Arthur has worked 11 days straight so far and is mandated for this weekend. He shared his shift did 70+ trailers today and they had 200+ coming in. He has never seen it this busy.

Chapter 10

Day 12

March 20, 2020, Friday

Beep, beep, beep.

I slapped the stupid alarm clock silent. I leaned over and kissed Joyce's exposed…upper thigh. Okay, that was different. I thought it was… You know what? Never mind. That wasn't important. What was important was that it was Friday! All right, I was looking forward to two days where I was not the one who was going to be the person who everyone was going to be looking for when something goes wrong.

The ride to work was just as lonely on the highway as it was the day before. Turning on the radio was just more chatter about who was or wasn't doing what to keep the pandemic from spreading. All I could think of about the ride in was how much I appreciated how I still had a job, how much I loved the kids and Joyce, and how terrifying this all was when you really thought about it. Luckily for the country, I didn't think all that much.

As I looked down at my lunch box after parking my truck in the parking lot, I saw that one of the gas masks that Joyce had asked me to get a while ago was sitting under the passenger seat of my truck. *Huh,* I thought, *so that is where that last one went.* Not thinking twice about it, I locked my truck and headed to the time clock.

The walk into work was chaotic, to say the least. Trucks were everywhere, forklifts were flying around with horns blaring, and the office was just a madhouse—you know, the "new" normal.

As I was flipping through some paperwork that was on my desk, I saw an official-looking memo on the clipboard for the morning pass-down for my shift.

"Hey, Jim," I asked quizzically, "what is this sheet on the pass-down for?"

"It's a list of questions we have to ask everyone at preshift. Anyone who answers yes needs to see a supervisor or HR," replied Jim.

As he was replying, I began reading to myself the questions:

1.   Have you been to an area defined by the CDC as a hot zone?
2.   Have you or anyone you know been tested for the COVID-19 virus?
3.   Have you or anyone you know tested positive for the COVID-19 virus?
4.   Are you feeling sick or showing signs of COVID-19?

Holding the paper in my hands, I just stared into space. This couldn't be happening. This couldn't possibly be happening. This was not a movie. This was not some sort of dream, was it? What was going on? Because right now, this looked like we were in the first act of a disaster film.

"Seriously? We seriously have to ask the guys this? Shouldn't a supervisor be asking these questions to the operators? Like, do any of these questions violate those damned HIPPO laws?" I asked with a tinge of disbelief.

"It's HIPPA, Art, HIPPA. And yeah, I thought the same thing when I saw it. And when you actually do find a supervisor, let me know so I can have him ask my shift. But seriously, though, what else are we going to do?" asked Jim.

"Yeah, amen to that. Good morning, boss," I said as Big Boss walked past me. "Did you see this? Do we really have to start asking these types of questions to the operators?"

"Yep, anyone who answers yes to any of those questions, you send straight to me. How do we look today, Jim?" asked Big Boss.

"Same as we have been doing, way too much work, not enough forklift operators, forklifts that have broken down, and an inventory guy that doesn't do anything around here," said Jim with a smile.

"You, sir, can go fly a kite. And when you do find someone who is dedicated solely to inventory, let me know because that is my job!" I replied.

"Thanks, Jim. Art, inventory might be your job, but remember, it is inventory plus other duties as assigned," replied Big Boss.

"Yeah, yeah. Big Boss, do you want to ask these questions for preshift?" I asked.

"No, it's yours. Other duties as assigned." Big Boss smirked.

Uuuggghhh. It was not necessarily that I was against asking these questions. In fact, they were probably a good thing to ask. But I was not a supervisor, and I did not have access to the time cards or had the power to grant vacation requests or whatever was needed at that level. Whatever. I kept my comments to myself and got ready to do the preshift meeting.

At the meeting was the normal crew, but because it was Friday, the weekend-shift guys were also here. Standing in front of me were some twenty-or-so grown men who I thought would be able to handle these questions. Who knew, right?

"Good morning, everyone," I started off. "Before we begin, I have been tasked with asking everyone the following questions. Have you been to an area defined by the CDC as a hot zone? Have you or anyone you know been tested for the COVID-19 virus? Have you or anyone you know tested positive for the COVID-19 virus? Are you feeling sick or showing signs of COVID-19?" As I put the paper in front of me down, I could start seeing the faces of everyone around me.

"*What kind of questions are those!*" yelled one operator.

"*What does* hot zone *mean?*" yelled another.

"Why should I tell you what my medical history or conditions are? Who are you to ask those, and why do you need to know?" yelled a third.

"I feel sick right now. Does that mean I can go home?" yelled another one of the guys.

"Go see Big Boss. Go see Big Boss. *Do you really feel sick? Go see Big Boss right now!"* was what I started yelling at everyone. Almost the whole crew started to bum-rush the office. Kurt, Wisecracker, and a few of the other forklift operators were standing off to the side, processing what was going on. I walked over to him.

"You okay, Kurt?" I asked.

"Who, me? Oh, I am fine, yea. I am not sick. I just can't believe what we are hearing. Some weird times right now," he replied.

"Yeah, tell me about it. Who knew that people were so afraid of their imminent mortality, right?" I asked morbidly, trying to crack a joke to ease the tension of everyone around me.

I did get a few slight chuckles, but those who didn't bum-rush Big Boss started to go about their day until Wisecracker heard a ding on his phone. Out of the corner of my eye, I watched him read whatever was sent to him, and his stance changed instantly. He looked up and stared at me and Kurt.

"What?" I asked.

"Yo, two people at another building just got sent home sick. With what, they don't know!" he replied.

Kurt and I just looked at each other.

"How do you know?" asked Kurt.

"When I went to the other site, I made friends with a supervisor. This guy is texting me right now!" said Wisecracker.

"You know what, Kurt, I will be right back," I said as I started walking away, remembering the gas mask that was in my truck.

"You're not leaving us, are you, Art?" asked Wisecracker.

"Please, you wish!" I replied.

I dodged pass the speeding forklifts to the nearest man door out of the building that led into the parking lot. Out in the parking lot, I dodged in the dark my way past the yard jockeys and tractor trailers to the employee parking spaces and opened the passenger-side door to my truck. I pulled out the gas mask and just stared at it. If I did this, there would be no going back until the pandemic was over. No one else was wearing a mask, so why should I? If I went in there with this mask on, people were going to either freak out or intimidate me by saying I was overreacting or whatever.

But Joyce was right about the gas masks being short on supply. She was right to be concerned about what was happening around us. This gas mask—it was what might be the difference between being sick and not sick. It was not doing anyone any good by just sitting on the floor of my truck. I opened up the package, put together the filter pieces, and secured them to the mask.

"Here we go, Arty boy," I said as I took a deep breath, held it, and pulled the mask over my face. I put my hand over the intake on the filter and made sure the seal was secure. It was… Nothing was getting in this thing. I started to try breathing normally. It was a little bit difficult, like trying to breathe with a towel over your face. But I adjusted how I was breathing, and it started to work okay. The mask itself, while it was supposed to be light, actually proved to be a little bit on the heavy side. It was awkward with the filters on my face, so my neck would have to get used to the weight. But I was going to have to try to make it work.

I grabbed the packaging, closed the door to my truck, and, as I walked across the parking lot, could see the yard jockeys and the truck drivers start to stare at me. I knew I probably looked like a walking spectacle to them, but I needed to keep myself as safe as possible. I was nervous. I didn't want to stand out, but I also didn't want to get sick. Even if I didn't get sick, I could still bring something home to Joyce, the kids, and my mother-in-law. After I successfully made it across the parking lot and to the building entrance, I put my badge up to the reader and opened the door.

In every forklift that drove by me, the operator just stared at me. I looked around to see if my vision was at all impeded. It wasn't. I could definitely see the forklift operators start to gather in small groups and make comments. You know what? To hell with them. I did not want to be the one to bring this virus to my family. They were locked down, and I was out here, exposed to everything. I had to, had to, *had to* do everything I could to keep all of us safe.

I walked into the office, and while no one spoke, they did stare. When I was walking toward my desk, Big Boss got a look at me.

"Art, don't you think this might be a little overkill?" said Big Boss.

"Boss," I said, muffled because you really couldn't hear people all that well through these things, "I cannot risk getting my babies or my mother-in-law getting sick. I don't care if other people are nervous because I am wearing this. They should be nervous. It's a pandemic. We are a week into this thing, and just because the government doesn't want to organize a response to this doesn't mean that I can't."

"Does it impede your vision at all? Can you work with it on?" asked Big Boss.

I handed him the packaging that just happened to have a picture of a construction worker using it. "It says it's OSHA certified to be safe, and it's not a full face mask. It's just a respirator. I can see and hear just fine. My voice is a little muffled, but you people don't like listening to me much anyway."

Big Boss looked at the packaging and then me. "If you can wear it and do your job, I don't have a problem with it."

"Thanks, boss," I said as I sat at my desk.

Everyone that drove by the office on their forklifts all stared. I got a little annoyed by all this, and given that I didn't have an email to answer, I decided that I was going to get some work done out on the warehouse floor. I gathered up my gear and got on my forklift. Then I realized that I had to use the restroom. Before I went over to the bathroom, I thought about Joyce and the kids.

Were they nervous or scared of me getting sick? Did they know that I was trying to protect myself as best as I could to keep everyone safe? I decided to send Joyce a message with a picture of me with my mask on just to try to make them feel a little better.

The rest of the day, beyond the gawking and the comments, went pretty much normally—juice in and juice out. Who on earth drinking all this juice was, was beyond me, but given that it was a struggle to even attempt to get toilet paper or disinfectant right now, I was not too surprised. The end of the day was going to be tough.

At the end of my shift, while I waited for Mark to clock in and do a pass-down with him, I stood by the time clock. With me were several of the other jockeys who I guess couldn't help themselves.

"Check it out, everyone. It's Art Vader," said one as they all broke into hysterics.

"Since when are you going into the hot zone?" asked another.

I politely smiled and just nodded my head. It's all fun and games until someone gets sick, and I was not going to be that guy. I mean, I usually was "that guy" a lot, but I didn't want to be "that guy" in this situation. The heckling and laughing continued when Mark walked in the door.

"Artemus," said Mark as he clocked in, "can you breathe normally with that on?"

"It's not terrible. But Mark, two people at the other building went home sick, and they don't know why. And now at preshift, you have to ask everyone questions about COVID-19," I replied.

"Oh my god, really! Yeah, I don't know. I am wondering if everyone is being really too relaxed about this pandemic stuff," said Mark. "How are the operations going?"

I gave Mark an overview of what inventory issues needed to get addressed and how the operations were doing from where I could see it: busy, very busy, very behind, short operators, short forklifts—you know, the usual.

After we were done talking, I headed to the time clock, clocked out, and headed toward my truck; and once inside, I took off my mask *finally* and started to drive home. While sitting at a stoplight, I was just observing the world around me when I immediately noticed something at the gas station at the other end of the intersection.

"What is this?" I muttered to myself. "Joyce has to see this! She hasn't left the house in almost two weeks!" I then got out my cell phone, took a picture, and sent it to Joyce. It was a picture of the sign at the gas station. Gas was $2.19 a gallon for regular.

Two dollars and nineteen cents a gallon for regular? I hadn't seen gas that cheap in a very long time. I mean, like, fifteen years ago, gas was that cheap, but wow, look at the price now! Well, I guessed there was at least one bright side to this pandemic!

I went to my mother-in-law's house first, worked on her coal stove, and said a quick hi, and then I headed to our house to work on ours. While I was downstairs, putting coal in the fireplace and taking out the ashes, I could hear Clara and Joyce running around upstairs, yelling, "*Daddy's here! Daddy's here!*" Boy, those little girls sure could make me smile.

After taking care of the coal stove, I went up to the hand sanitizer zip-tied to the deck and started putting some on my hands when Joyce and the kids came outside.

"Daddy!" yelled Clara.

"Hey, princesses, were you good for Mom while I was at work?" I asked.

"Yes, they were both good. I showed them the picture of you at work with your gas mask on. Did it freak a lot of people out?" asked Joyce.

"Yeah, there were some comments made, but when I heard of people being sent home for being sick for unknown reasons and people during preshift saying that they didn't feel good and wanted to go home, I decided that I needed to start protecting myself," I said.

"You did the right thing, Art. Those masks aren't doing anyone any good while they are just sitting in the package," said Joyce.

"That is exactly what I thought! Did you see the picture of the gas station?" I asked.

"Yeah, that's nuts! Were all the gas stations that cheap?" asked Joyce.

"No," I said, "that was the cheapest that I saw, but the others on the way home weren't too far off. Why do you think it is so low?"

"Well, my car gets one month to the gallon now, so I imagine there are a ton of other people doing the same thing that I am," said Joyce. "Come on, I have dinner ready."

We all went inside and had dinner, talking about how the days were going. The news was background noise while we chatted. Because of what we were doing, it was sort of nice, but at the same time, it was amazing to me that the kids were completely isolated by what was going on around them. I didn't know if they really had a sense of what was going on, *thank God*. My job and Joyce's job was to protect them, and they were so little. Did they really need to know?

After dinner, we went out into the yard and played badminton. Yeah, I was tired, and yeah, I was achy, but Peanut was doing really well at it. And she loved playing with me. How could I say no? Clara continued to just barrel-roll down the hill while Joyce was in the porch swing, watching us. I just happened to look up as I went to serve a birdie, and I missed it.

"What's wrong, Dad?" asked Joyce. She had noticed that I was still looking up.

"Joyce, hon, look up," I said. "What do you see?"

"Nothing, Dad. Why?" she said.

"Yeah, what are you looking at, Dad?" asked Joyce from the porch swing.

"Look how clear the sky is. There is nothing up there, and doesn't the sky look, I don't know, a little clearer?" I said. To me it was, like, less cloudy and hazy.

"Hey, Mom, Dad is right!" said Peanut.

It was a sight that I had not seen since 9/11. The sky was unusually clear. Even a color-blind guy could see that. No planes were in the sky either, not even a little prop plane from the small local airport down in Wyoming. Everything was very still up in the sky. It also meant to me that no one was moving and that no freight was moving by plane. No wonder the price of gas had fallen. The lockdown, no matter what everyone thought about how effective it was or not, was having an actual tangible effect that you could see. Wow, just wow.

After we were done playing, the kids went inside, and I joined Joyce on the porch swing with a drink to yell at cars that drove by.

"Joyce, have I had a chance to tell you that I think that you are the most beautiful woman in the world and that I am so happy that I married you?" I asked after a spirited yell at a car that just drove by.

"I love you too," said Joyce. "How was everyone at work with you wearing your mask?"

"Pretty much everyone made fun of it," I answered. "But I don't care. I want to try to do everything I can to keep us safe. What do you think of it?"

"I love you, and I think you are doing the right thing. I know it is hard on you to have to wear it at work all the time. I am sorry that you have to do it," she said.

I nodded and went back to yelling at cars and looking at the sky. In the meantime, I reached my hand out to her, and she took it. We sat quietly for a bit longer, just doing that until it started to get a little late and cold.

We got into the house and cleaned up for the night. I told Joyce that I would get the kids ready for bed and headed up to the upstairs bathroom. When I got upstairs, I got the kids' stuff ready for them to go to bed—you know, putting toothpaste on their little toothbrushes, getting their vitamins and fluoride ready, and then calling them to get their pj's on and get ready for bed.

"But, Daaad, I want to play video games," cried Clara.

"Yeah, we are in the middle of this game we're playing," said Joyce.

"I know, princesses. But it's time for bed, and Daddy is tired. Is there any way you guys can save your games?" I asked.

Little Joyce nodded and saved the game that they were both were playing while Clara stomped her way into the bathroom.

"Dad, can Clara sleep in my room tonight?" asked Joyce.

"Sure, sweetie, I don't see a problem with that," I replied, and I really didn't have a problem with it. Normally, what happened was if Clara woke up in the middle of the night, she'd go into Joyce's room and cuddle with her anyway.

After they finished brushing their teeth and getting ready, we all piled into little Joyce's bed. As we began to watch a little TV and turned off the lights, I noticed Clara cuddling Joyce and Joyce cuddling Clara as they drifted off to sleep. The sight was just too adorable, though, so I felt I really had to say something.

"Joyce, Clara, Daddy loves you very much. And I know times are really weird right now, so I really appreciate you guys being good for Mom and me. We both love you so much," I said.

Clara lifted her head up and looked at me. "I love you too, Dad, but you're not as cool as Uncle Brian."

Ugh, Elizabeth!

Joyce, while still cuddling Clara, turned around and looked at me. "Me too. I love you too, Dad."

I lay with them for a while until I was pretty sure they were both asleep. I then snuck out and went into my and Joyce's bedroom to go right to sleep, but when I opened the door, I found Joyce in the bed, slowly drifting to sleep too.

I got into bed and stroked her hair while we silently watched TV. It was *a struggle* to stay away long enough and to continue stroking her hair and not slap her in the head while I started dozing off, but as far as I could remember, I was able to pull it off. That night, if there was a race for who was going to fall asleep first, I think we would have tied.

Joyce's Journal

Friday, March 20, 2020

Restless night last night. This morning's news is reporting some law makers sold off millions of $ of shares of stock before markets dropped but were saying how well off our country will be. Some were democrats, some republicans. Husband sent picture from work. He is now wearing his respirator. A few people in the industrial park have been sent home sick.

NY mayor—April will jump in cases. Hotels near hospitals will become temporary places to treat patients. He stated we need supplies, medical. "Where is the federal government?"

Chapter 11

Day 13: The Second Weekend

March 21, 2020, Saturday

Beep, beep, beep.

I slapped the stupid alarm clock silent again for another day, another consecutive day. Boy, this was getting tiring. I leaned over and gave Joyce a kiss on the forehead. "I love you," I whispered to her before I left—another morning of the new normal.

I made myself coffee and got my lunch ready for the day. You know, it took me about twenty minutes to get ready and go. I wondered if anyone would hear if the TV was on. Why risk it, though? It was three-thirty in the morning. Did I really want to wake up the entire house? As long as I didn't trip on either of the dogs and make them yelp, I would be good.

I got out the door, managed not to hurt the dogs, and got in my truck. This ride to work, though, would be different. I would admit that there was a tiny bit more truck traffic this morning, but that was not what caught my eye.

Over the past few years, PennDOT had been installing these giant lighted information signs. For the most part, they basically conveyed either imminent traffic delays, missing children, Amber Alert information, or sometimes a holiday greeting. But as I came from a distance, I muttered to myself, "What does it say this morning?" When I saw it, it took a second for me to register.

"No," I said to myself, "it didn't say that. Did it really say that? Did it really, really, *really* say that?"

I had already passed the sign when I decided to pull over to get a better look at the same sign, which faced the northbound lanes of I-81. I pulled over my truck, got out, and took a picture.

"Stay home and limit travel" was what the sign kept flashing at everyone driving by that could read it. The government was actually telling us to stay home and limit travel. Like, *seriously, all you people out right now need to stay home and not move because this is a serious virus*! At the moment, all I saw traveling about me were "essential" employees and trucks.

As I pulled into the parking lot, there was the same number of trucks as the day before—figures. Though, I did notice that there were actually a few opened parking spots. What gives? Did we not have enough work for everyone? Did they cancel some of the mandatory overtime and not tell me? I would love nothing more right now than to be home with Joyce and the kids, but no, I was here at 5:00 a.m.

Already with a chip in my shoulder, I clocked into work and began walking toward the office. Forklifts were sitting off to one side. They were not red-tagged Out of Service or anything; they were just not being used. How the heck could that possibly be? I went over to one and ensured that there were no personal items on it or anything and that no one had been logged into it already.

It wasn't being used. *Awesome!* I quickly logged in to the computer with my sign-on, and on my way down to the office I went. I wasn't going to be shackled to the desk today; I would get to actually load some trucks and get some work done! This was going to be great. At least that was what I thought at first anyway.

I pulled up to the office and saw Calieb at the dispatcher's desk as usual. I hopped off the machine and jovially walked in.

"Yo, Calieb, guess you cancelled the overtime because I got a lift, so we gonna be good today, brother!" I yelled.

Calieb just stared blankly up at me and got up from his desk. He began walking toward Big Boss's office, motioning me to follow him. When he got to Big Boss's desk, he grabbed a stack of papers and then started flipping through them.

"I don't know what you are so excited about. Half of the shifts are calling off. They are not coming in. So yeeaaah, it is nice that you have a forklift, but now we have three times the work. So let's hold off on canceling all that overtime, shall we?" he said as he handed me a paper.

I took it from him. "What is that?" I asked as I began reading it.

"It's a letter from the corporate HR department, essentially a permission slip so you can go to work," he replied.

"Who would need this? For, like, if they ever declared martial law?" I asked, sort of confused.

"When there is a lockdown, law enforcement or military may set up checkpoints along major transportation routes, so I guess it's like martial law. Anyone caught a checkpoint without any documents is sent home. This is to prove to them that you are an essential employee here and that you need to get to work," said Calieb as he returned to his desk.

The letter read,

> To whom it may concern:
>
> This document denotes that the bearer of the document is an employee and is considered an employee of an essential business or is providing services to an essential business. The team member performs work which is vital to keeping the community supplied. If you have any questions please contact...

How much more was going to happen! I quickly took a picture of the letter and sent it to Joyce and the chief of police in our town. I then walked up behind Calieb to take the first truck to do.

"So you ready to do some trucks?" he asked.

I smiled and said, "Now that I have my permission slip, I do. Why did we get people calling off?"

"I don't know," he said. "Maybe they are afraid to work overtime or they are burned out. Who knows? What we do know is that they are not here, so our job just got that much harder."

"Well then," I said, "less talky and more worky."

I got onto my forklift and started to work. Basically, for the next few hours, that's what I did, but mostly outbound trucks. We were shipping out sooo much juice. I did maybe, *maybe*, one or two inbound trucks. But for the most part, what we had to do as far as work was we had to ship out waaay more trucks than we had to do in. Over the past week, I had noticed little by little our warehouse was starting to get emptier and emptier. I wondered how long it was going to be before we were down to our last pallets of juice. And then what?

I finished out my day, said goodbye to Calieb, and clocked out. I wanted to stop on the way home for maybe a slushy from the convenience store. Normally, when I worked overtime, I would stop for gas, and I'd usually get a slushy because it just got me through until I could get home, you know? I would work all day, just thinking about how delicious it would be. But that was in the before times, like, two weeks ago—before they shut everything down and we weren't terrified of our groceries. I wouldn't dare step foot inside the convenience store up here in Mountain Top now. I just kept on driving by, sadly.

I got home, did the normal routine with the coal stoves and telling the kids to not hug Daddy until I got a shower, and washed myself down with sanitizer—you know, the usual. As I was coming out of the shower, I didn't hear Joyce come into the bathroom, and there she was before me. Was this a nice surprise?

"Well, hello there, miss. I know your husband isn't home. Is there something that I can help you with?" I said seductively.

"Stop it," Joyce said authoritatively. "We are low on milk, and the kids have been cooped up in here for almost a week. Can we take a drive down to the dairy store in West Pittston and get a couple of gallons of milk and maybe some ice cream?"

Welp, back to work.

"Sure, hon," I said while drying off. "Let me put on a change of clothes. Is it okay if we take your car? It hasn't moved in, like, two weeks."

"Yeah, we can take my car. Would you mind wearing your mask into the store?" asked Joyce.

I had to think about that for a second. Wearing a mask at work was no problem because it was work, but wearing a mask out in public, looking like I was trying to rob the place? Is that something I was ready to do? I was looking at Joyce the entire time I was thinking all of this, and I knew that I couldn't. I just couldn't ask her to do it and put her in harm's way.

"Sure, honey," I said, at the same time trying to hide that I was swallowing my fear of what I was about to do. "Do you want to get the kids ready?"

"They are already waiting. Just need you, dear," said Joyce as she left the room. I got downstairs, and the kids were both ready to go.

"We're going for a ride, Mommy?" asked Clara.

"Yep, you guys ready to go?" replied Joyce.

"Yaaaaaa!" gleed Peanut and Clara.

We all rushed out of the house to Joyce's car and got in. I opened my truck up and got my new respirator out.

"What is that, Daddy?" asked Peanut.

"It's Daddy's new mask that I have to wear at work so that I don't get sick," I said.

"You look like a spaceman, Dad!" said Clara.

"Hon, at the moment, I feel like I go to the moon every time I leave the house!" I said more as a comment about how much the world has changed and was starting to become unrecognizable rather than a joke.

"Daddy's a moon man!" both of the kids yelped.

As I started to drive it, you could hear the car groan as it moved for the first time in weeks. Joyce and I looked at each other as we heard the tires break free and move as I started to drive in reverse. "Maybe it would be a good idea for you to take my car every once and a while so this thing doesn't just completely seize up," Joyce said.

"Good call," I said as I started driving toward West Pittston.

The dairy store, which was an ice-cream parlor and dairy, was about twenty minutes away. While it didn't seem like much before the virus, the kids were thrilled just to get out of the house and see the world again. Every now and then, I would watch them in the mirror, and they didn't talk much. They just watched all the houses and trees go flying by as we made our way downtown. Another thing I guessed that I was taking for granted was the daily change in scenery. It made me feel a little bit worse inside, knowing that I was the only one in the house that got to break up the monotony of the day.

We pulled into the parking lot, and so far, it looked like we were the only ones there. *Thank God.*

"You ready?" asked Joyce as she handed me my respirator.

"Yeah, I will be okay. You kids stay here and be good for Mom, okay?" I said to the girls.

"Okay, Dad," said Peanut.

"Bye, Daddy. Where you going?" asked Clara.

"Daddy is going to get some milk and ice cream," Joyce said to Clara as I was putting on my mask. "Okay, get three gallons of whole milk, one gallon of 2 percent milk, and some ice cream, something everyone will like, so just chocolate or vanilla, okay? No crazy flavors like you usually get."

I nodded and stepped out of the car. I swore I felt like I was traveling through a war zone, trying to get to the creamery. I opened up the door, and inside there were two female teenage workers. They both looked at me, and instantly I did not get a good vibe. I probably should make it quick. As fast as I could, I grabbed the four gallons of milk from the display and put them on the counter in front of one of the girls.

"I will be right back. I need some ice cream," I said in a muffled voice that struggled to get out of the mask.

The poor girl, and I felt bad for her. I really did. She was either scared or confused, or both. She just nodded her head as I made my way over to the ice cream. The nice thing about this place was that they actually sold half gallons of ice cream instead of pints. The rest of the liberal ice-cream industry seemed to have shifted. They sold you less for the same price, which I guess worked, but you ended up having to get it more often. Not these people, though—they just raised the price of their ice cream, and I was fine with that.

I picked vanilla and went back to the counter where the girl rang my order up. I handed her more money than I needed and told her, "Keep the change." That made her feel a little better as she smiled, and I left. I was trying to be nice, yeah, but really, I just didn't want to get any change back because what if the virus could be spread around through the money?

I left the shop and came out with my provisions. While I was in there, a car pulled up right next to ours, and the people had not gotten out yet. While I started walking toward the car, Joyce saw that I had come out. She stepped out with sanitizer wipes and hand sanitizer. We began wiping down the jugs of milk and the ice cream while the people in the car next to us just stared. When we were done, Joyce got back into the passenger seat while I worked on closing up the back of her car. In the meantime, the people in the car next to us got out of their car. They were an elderly couple, and the husband, who had gotten out of his door first, just locked eyes with me. I nodded to him behind my mask, but I don't know if he was angry, shocked, or jealous. Whatever, this is the new world now, buddy.

We left there with what we came down for. Plus, we knew that right now, we were definitely in the minority of people who were doing what we were supposed to be doing. Other folks either didn't care or were not taking this seriously. Well, that was them, and this was us. The safety of Joyce and the kids took priority above everything else.

We got home and unloaded everything. By the time we were finished, I was beat. With everyone just kind of putzing around in the kitchen, I figured that it would be okay to get everyone ready for bed. I really needed to head to bed.

"Joyce, do you have a problem with me putting the kids to sleep?"

"Oh, come on, why do we have to go to bed? Can we please stay up? It's Saturday!" said little Joyce.

"Yeah, Mom, can we please stay up with you?" asked Clara.

I saw the look in Joyce's eyes. It was one of "Oh, come on, please, can I have a few seconds to myself?"

"No, girls," I said. "You guys can watch TV, and we can all snuggle in Joyce's bed. If I start to fall asleep, just keep the noise down."

"Dad's right," a seemingly relieved Joyce said. "You guys need to go to sleep. Thanks, Artie."

"You got it, hon. Joyce, have I had a chance to tell you today that I think that you are the most beautiful woman in the world and that I am so happy that I married you?" I said as I picked up Clara.

"I love you too. Good night, guys!"

"Good night!" Joyce, Clara, and I all said at the same time. With that, I took the girls upstairs to get changed, get their clothes on, and get their teeth brushed. After that, we all snuggled together in Peanut's bed and watched some TV. After a while, I did fall asleep before the kids, but at around midnight, I had woken up. Both of the girls were sound asleep. I groggily got out of the bed and made my way to my bed. I was so tired I couldn't keep my eyes opened, so I just felt my way to my bed.

I crawled in and went to look at my alarm clock. It looked like Joyce had already set it for the right time. I felt around in the bed and found her lying with her back to me. She must have come up sometime during the night. I patted her back, closed my eyes, and fell asleep.

Joyce's Journal

Saturday, March 21, 2020

Picked up mom's car at garage. Way too many people still wandering/driving around. Arthur picked up milk (I froze one of them) and ice cream. He wore his respirator into the creamery.

This morning he sent me a picture of his permission/identification of being an essential employee of the state. Makes you wonder if they shut down roads and only let essentials move around.

It's Saturday, so no schoolwork. Arthur still working every day.

Day 14

March 22, 2020, Sunday

Beep, beep, beep.

I slapped the stupid alarm clock silent again for another day, another consecutive day. Boy, this was getting tiring. I leaned over and gave Joyce a kiss on the… *What? Come on, where are you?* Elbow—I found her elbow. I gave Joyce a kiss on the elbow and whispered, "I love you," to her before I left—another morning of the new normal.

Getting ready and the drive into work was basically the same as it had been as of late. What was *not* the same was the number of trucks waiting to get into the building. It was much less than before. It was noticeable. I mean, yeah, there were still *a lot* of trucks waiting to get worked, *but* the line wasn't coming out of the parking lot. *Thank God.*

I got into the employee parking lot, and again, there were a few cars less than there should be. Walking into the building, clocking in, and getting to the office, I noticed that there was a noticeable decrease in the amount of traffic. There was even a forklift for me to use. How cool was that?

"Good morning, Calieb," I said as I went to grab some paperwork for trucks. "Some people call off again? And is our volume down? I saw that there were quite a few less trucks waiting to get in here from the road."

"Yeah, the volume is lighter today, and because of all the outbounds, we have so much room in here that we're doing the inbounds faster. And you won't guess who I got a text message from, saying that they won't be in tomorrow and will try to come in during the week sometime," said Calieb.

I was nervous to even ask. "Do I want to know who is calling off? Are they okay? Do they have the virus?" I asked.

"Big Boss sent me a text. It is not COVID-19 related, but he won't be coming in," said Calieb.

"Oh no," I kind of stammered out.

Calieb nodded his head, and I took my paperwork and went back to my forklift. There was no support now. It was just me and the dispatcher on our shift. I thought, *God, please don't let this last very long.* You know, because right now, his top priority was making sure that I didn't have a lot of stress. We can do okay for a short period without Big Boss, but we have no one to address personnel issues or anything that requires authorization above me, and there can be a lot of things that can go wrong. I guessed we would just have to do everything we could to keep it all going and just wait to answer the question of "What gives you the authority to?" later.

That was basically the big news on that Sunday. That the situation just got harder for the week coming up. More people were probably going to be burned out, so more call-offs. At least the volume was going down. I mean, arguably, the amount of people we had working was also going down, so nothing was really going to change that much. But hey…the volume was going down.

While I was waiting to clock out at the end of the day, Mark walked up behind me. "Another busy day, Artemus?"

I turned around. "Yeah, but the amount of trucks waiting is down, so it's getting slightly better."

"Yea," replied Mark, "I saw that coming in. Do we have work left for the second shift?"

"Oooh, yes, and Calieb told me this morning that Big Boss called off tomorrow but will try to be in sometime this week," I said.

"Nooo, that means it's just going to be you?" asked Mark.

"Yep, I would ask if you could come in earlier, but you are already staying later. So we're just going to have to, you know, deal with it," I said as I clocked out. "See you tomorrow, Mark."

"You know it, buddy. Have a safe trip home," he said.

And with that, I was out the door. I rushed home, did my routine, and tried to do everything quicker so that I could be with Joyce and the kids for a while before I had to go to work…again. After playing with the kids for a while, Joyce called us for dinner. While eating, I broke the news to Joyce.

"So this morning, Calieb told me that Big Boss is calling off on Monday but will try to be in sometime during the week," I said while picking up a forkful of food.

"Wait, so there is no manager or supervisor? Who takes care of, like, payroll or anything?" asked Joyce. My guess was that she was concerned that no one would be looking to make sure I got paid for all this overtime I was working.

"The only things that I can't do are the payroll and work on personnel issues like vacations or employee conflicts or anything like that. I am not a supervisor and don't have access to the systems or reports. Figuring out how many people we're going to need to work, prioritizing loads, or whatever, I will be able to do with the dispatcher. The payroll stuff is automatic I think, or someone at corporate will be looking at it. At least I hope so."

Before I was in inventory control, I spent a year as a dispatcher. It was a fun job, but I got tired being behind the desk all day. At least in inventory, half your day was spent being at the desk while the other half was spent working on the warehouse floor.

"The only problem with me not being a supervisor is if I ask someone to do something, they can tell me no, and there really isn't anything that I can do about it."

"Listen, mister, you just go to work, do your job the best you can, then come home to me and the kids," said Joyce. She had been saying this for ten-plus years every time I worried or complained about work. And every time I heard it, I knew she is right.

"Joyce, did I have a chance to tell you today that I think that you are the most beautiful woman in the world and that I am so happy that I married you?"

"I love you too. Are you going to put the kids to bed again?" asked Joyce.

"Yeah, I think I can manage that. How were the girls for you today?" I said while I went to take a sip of water.

"The girls had a little fight but are playing really well together. It is so hard on them, being cooped up inside the house. I just wish the weather was a little warmer so they could go outside and play.

They have all this bottled-up energy, and playing video games and painting only goes so far," Joyce lamented.

While I had been at work these past few weeks, Joyce had been doing some sort of school-related projects to keep Peanut on task so she would not forget anything she had learned since the classes shut down. Clara had been doing a lot of painting with the water paints to keep herself occupied. Joyce gave both the girls a section of a wall in the house (Clara's was in the kitchen, and little Joyce's was in the living room) that they filled with their "artings" every day to be displayed. One of the things that I really hadn't talked about was how much I appreciated seeing all the paintings. I mean, being color-blind, I might never really get to appreciate *all* the colors that they used or made, but keeping the kids occupied and involved was a great way to keep them from dwelling on what was going on in the world around them.

"Yeah, I know. If it gets warmer out during the week, I will have to think of a place that I could take them to maybe ride bikes. The last time it was nice out, I took the kids over to Frances Slocum, and that didn't turn out all that great," I said, thinking about what happened last week when I took them.

"I will try to think of a place too. If I think of one, I will let you know," said Joyce.

Joyce's Journal

Sunday, March 22, 2020

NY gov. daily briefing, 4–6 months? We don't know. Still saying 40–80% will get sick. Arthur still working every day. His 14th day straight.

I listened to a reporter do an interview, and the person being interviewed stated, "This president should stop lying, making jokes, and tell the truth."

I had eggs for breakfast. So yummy!!! Kids are busy and relaxing right now.

Chapter 12

Day 15: Mondays and Tuesdays

March 23, 2020, Monday

Beep, beep, beep.

With one eye glaring at the blasted machine that woke me every…single…morning, I reached out and, instead of striking it with a final blow, gently tapped it silent. Maybe I should be nice to it today. It was not the clock's fault that I had to get up early to go to work. Also, without fail, it did a great job of getting me out of the bed for the day. Okay, so today, *and only today*, I would be nice to my alarm clock. Before I rolled out of bed, though, I gave Joyce a quick kiss on the back of her head. "I love you," I whispered. She seemed to move a little bit and whispered back, "I love you too. I have to go to the bathroom."

I chuckled. "Go ahead. You go first. I will go use the downstairs bathroom."

"Thank you," she said as I left the room.

I got downstairs, got ready, and got into work without any real problems. The number of trucks waiting to be loaded was about the same as it was the day prior, but given that this was Monday and not the weekend, that was very promising to me. Maybe, *just maybe*, people had started to horde less juice, and we could finally have a chance to breathe.

After clocking in, the first person that I wanted to talk to was Calieb, who was in the office with Jim. Before I had a chance to ask

Calieb, who must have sensed what I wanted to know first, the first words out of his mouth were the answer.

"This weekend is not going to be mandatory, not at first anyway, if that is what you are going to ask me," said Calieb with a smile.

"Thank goodness," I said, relieved. "You have no idea how much I am relieved by this."

"Yeah, don't get too excited yet. I didn't finish with what I wanted to tell you," said Calieb.

I knew it was too good to be true. "What? What could possibly ruin that news?"

"We are going to ask that everyone to at least volunteer to do one day this weekend. If not enough people volunteer, *then* the shifts will be mandated. So congrats, you aren't mandated, but if you don't volunteer, then you will have to work," said Calieb with that smile disappearing.

"Uggghhh, is that what Big Boss said?" I asked.

"Yeah, he sent me a text after I let him know what our volume for the week is going to be," replied Calieb.

"Welp, I hope we get enough people to volunteer," I said.

"Are you going to?" asked Calieb.

"Yeah, probably," I said. "As long as I get at least one day off this weekend, that would be very nice."

"Yea. Oh, also, were you expecting any big-box store returns?" asked Calieb.

Instantly the hair on my neck stood up. "Yeah, why?"

"There are five of them in the yard right now. We didn't know what to do with them, and instead of tying up the stage locations on the docks, we decided to just leave them in the yard," said Calieb as he handed me the paperwork for each of them.

"There are five *here already*!" I shrieked as I flipped through the paperwork. I got why the weekend shift did that; there was no one else here that could work them. So basically, yeah, the trailers were waiting for me. "Can we get these in a door? You don't have to give all five at once. Just dedicate one door all morning long, and I will get them done."

"Got it," said Calieb.

At the preshift meeting, I let everyone know that Big Boss was out and that we needed people to volunteer at least one day during the weekend to avoid everyone getting mandated for a third weekend in a row. For the most part, everyone nodded and agreed. A few people complained, but more than likely, they wouldn't show up anyway. Couldn't say that I blamed them, but I couldn't imagine what it would be like here the day after Mark or I called off.

And of course, Wisecracker had to say something: "So if Big Boss isn't here, does that mean that you are in charge?"

Ugh, I guess me saying that I was not a supervisor and that this wasn't my shift was about to come back to haunt me.

"I am not saying that I am in charge, *but* I am saying that I will not let this place fail. If I ask you to do something, you can tell me no, and since I am not a supervisor, I can't write you up. But I know who can write you up and when they come back you can talk to them. So I guess what I am saying is that the world right now is at the mercy of everyone's own moral compass. You all know here that I will do everything that I can to help you and to keep things moving as quickly and easily as possible, but we will all need to work together on this. Any other questions?"

"So just making sure, you can't write us up for telling you no?" asked Wisecracker.

"Everyone, be safe and get to work," I smiled and replied.

After the meeting, I started working the returns. While I was doing that, every time someone was missing a pallet, had damage, or had a discrepancy on the count of their pallet; a truck needed to be checked; or someone had a problem with an inbound or whatever, I was being pulled away to do that task. Kurt and some of the other more-experienced operators did help wherever they could, and it was a big help. But there was still plenty for me to do. My own personal goal was that if I started working on a problem, I had to fix it because I was not going to leave Mark with a bunch of loose ends to fix from my shift.

Having all the work to do did help my day go by faster. I didn't even really notice that it was time to go until I felt my stomach start to rumble because I missed lunch. I looked up at the clock and was relieved to see that it was time to go. Luckily, I had finished up my last problem, and there were no loose ends for Mark. I made my way up to the time clock, and instead of waiting for Mark, I had to use the restroom.

By the time I was I finished and came out of the bathroom, I saw Mark walking down the docks toward the offices. I normally would yell to him or chase him down to let him know what was going on, but I was just so drained of energy at this point that I just said, "Meh," and figured anything that was vitally important, he would read in one of my emails. At least I hope people read my emails.

I headed home and did the new routine: coal stove, coal stove, sanitize, hug kids! I didn't see Joyce when I walked in; she was in the downstairs bathroom. So I went upstairs to decontaminate first before giving the kids their hugs. They were so eager to see me sometimes. It was so cute!

"Were you girls good for Mom today?" I asked when I came down from taking my shower, and they were waiting for me in the living room to give me a hug. They both came up to me with big smiles, still in their pj's.

"Yeah, we were good. Hey, Dad, no more school for another two weeks!" yelped little Joyce.

I was puzzled. "Just another two weeks?"

"Ha," I heard Joyce laugh from behind me. "Yeah, it's just another two weeks from what they say. I don't know, though, Artie. I think it's going to be a lot longer than that."

I released the kids from their hugs to let them go back to playing their games and went over to Joyce in the kitchen, who was making everyone dinner.

"Why?" I asked.

"Why what? Do you really think during a pandemic that we are just going to throw the kids back into the schools to spread whatever this is to everyone even faster? The governor right now is just stalling for time so people don't get upset at him. It's a national emergency. No one is going anywhere anytime soon. We need to get out of this mindset that we are just going to magically go back to our normal lives after one or two weeks," she said, a little bit more excitedly than usual.

"Well, I am not disagreeing with you, but how are we going to keep teaching the kids?" I asked.

"This isn't something where we can just switch to cyber schooling for the district, Arthur. This isn't normal operations. This is crisis learning. What happens if one of these kid's parents is sick and we do switch to cyber schooling? Do they think the teachers are going to follow up with the kids if they don't turn in their work? Some of the kids rely on the school for their food. What about them? The last thing we need to do right now is worry about someone's essay assignment," said Joyce, getting progressively more passionate as she talked. It is pretty obvious that this was something that had been eating at her for a little bit.

"Ugh, I don't know, hon. I just don't know. I do know that, Joyce, have I had a chance to tell you today that I think you're the most beautiful woman in the world and that I am so happy that I married you?" I said.

"I love you too, but, well, I know that our kids will be fine. I am ordering some workbooks for Joyce to get her through the rest of the year if the district doesn't figure out what it wants to do and quick. It's not like it's their fault. It's is no one's fault. Who would have ever seen a global pandemic coming and shutting everything down? But we need to act now and quickly if we are going to be able to help all these kids," said Joyce as she finished making dinner.

I called the kids down for dinner, and we all sat down and watched the news. The stay-at-home orders, handed out a little while ago, were affecting communities everywhere. People who were living paycheck to paycheck with no savings were really struggling. I mean, we were not in the best shape, but we did have a meager amount of savings to hold us over in case something serious happened. But money only has as much power as we give it, so if the government would only pass some sort of emergency economic relief for people, we could help society as a whole. But for some reason, they didn't want to pass a stimulus bill yet. This was going to get a lot worse before it got better.

"How was work?" asked Joyce as we cleaned up after dinner. "Are you going to be mandated this weekend?"

"Well, when I went into work today, I told them, 'Team, I have not seen my family in more than two weeks. I did not sign up for this, so I am taking one day off this weekend, end of story.'" I replied.

"Uh-huh," said a skeptical Joyce. "What really happened?"

"Calieb got a text this morning from Big Boss," I said.

"The weekend shift supervisor?" asked Joyce.

"Yeah, but he works third shift. Mondays and Fridays too. Anyway, he got a text after we sent him the workload for the week, and he said that there is no mandatory work for this weekend."

"That's great. So you are going to get to have this weekend off?" Joyce asked excitedly.

"Well, wait, I wasn't finished. The weekend isn't going to be mandated, but we have to volunteer to work at least one day this weekend. I told them that I was willing to work Saturday but that I wanted Sunday off," I said.

Joyce got a little disappointed. "Oh, well, you're going to get at least one day off."

"Daddy is going to have off this weekend? You won't have to work?" asked Peanut as she came running in from the living room, holding her video game.

I turned around and picked her up. "Yep, princess, it looks like daddy is going to get to have a day off!"

Clara came running in next and up into Daddy's arms. Now I was holding both of the girls. "Daddy no have to work this weekend?"

"If Daddy doesn't absolutely have to… No, I will have a day off this weekend." I said happily.

The mood in the room got a little more optimistic, and while I held both kids, Joyce came over and gave us all a big hug. Finally, *finally*, something to look forward too. Today was Monday, so all I had to do was make it, what, five more days? This was going to be a piece of cake.

Joyce's Journal

Monday, March 23, 2020

The children woke up late today. It is what it is. I got to sleep in as well. Daily update from Gov. (NY) Surgeon General warns, "This week, it's going to get bad."

Senate did not pass stimulus bill yet. Very worried with people not working, how this is affect our communities. People have begun sewing cloth masks. This is nice, but I wonder why has the president not used defense act to ramp up production. He still has not done this. NY gov., all hospitals need to increase capacity by 50%.

Evening, Monday—no stimulus bill yet. Held up because not enough funds to bail out businesses.

PA gov. extended school closure additional 2 weeks. April 13 would be the new return date. I do not think we will go back that early.

Day 16

March 24, 2020, Tuesday

Beep, beep, beep.

Bam! I smacked the alarm clock silent. *No more being nice with you.* I leaned over, gave Joyce a kiss on her forehead, and whispered, "I love you." Still fast asleep, she didn't really move. I slowly and quietly got out of bed so she wouldn't wake up, and with that, the day had started.

The morning routine seemed to go by quickly, and as I was driving into work, the news radio said that the automotive industry, under the direction of the president with authority given to him by some sort of emergency defense act, was going to start making ventilators to help out the hospitals. The automotive industry making ventilators? In my mind, I started picturing the commercials and the jingles for that:

Have you breathed in a Fooord lately?

I love how you breathe for me, Toyota!

Upside-down ventilators, it's a Jeep thing.

I know that some of you younger readers, born before 2000, won't get those jingles. Go on whatever Internet website you're using now to look up 1990s car commercials, then you will get it.

I got into work—busy, still busy. It was not as insane as it was a week ago, but it was still busy. I parked my truck and went to clock in. As I clocked in, Kurt drove by on a forklift.

"Good morning, Mr. Art!" said Kurt.

"Good morning, Kurt. Are we busy today?" I asked, knowing that Kurt came in about an hour before me and talked to Jim.

"Yes, very. Where is Big Boss?" asked Kurt.

"Well, I didn't get any texts from him, and he knows that I am the only on—" I was interrupted by a *ping* on my cell phone—a text. Kurt and I both looked at each other.

"Who is that from?" asked Kurt.

I got my phone out of my pocket. It was from Big Boss.

"It is from Big Boss. 'Art, sorry I am not going to be in today or the rest of the week. Contact Calieb for any immediate help.'" I read out loud from my phone. I looked at Kurt and said, "You just had to jinx it, didn't you?"

Kurt let out a laugh. "I didn't do it, I swear. That's okay, Art. I know that you are going to do a great job."

"You too, Kurt," I said as I kept on walking toward the office. As I walked in, Jim was extremely busy.

"Hey, I need you to help me," said Jim without even so much as a *good morning* to me first as he handed me two inbound trucks that had problems.

"I got you, buddy," I said as I took them from him and started working. "Do we have any customer returns in the yard?"

"No, not yet. If I get one, do you want me to put it to a door?" he asked.

"Do we have any doors for you to put them in?" I asked.

He just smirked at me then said, "What do you think?"

"Probably not. We're pretty busy at the moment. You can hold off on the returns if they show up. If I have to, I will leave one or two for Mark. I don't want to do that, though, because his shift has slightly weaker forklift operators, so the less that I leave for him the more help he can give to his guys," I said as I went to work.

The time was flying by pretty good at work until about 11:00 a.m., I want to say.

"Art, this is Kurt. Do you copy?" I heard on the radio while I was fixing a pallet stuck in the racks.

"Yeah, go ahead, Kurt," I replied.

"Art, can you come down to the aisle I am in? I was driving to my truck, and I found a pallet in a location that, well, it's in pretty bad shape, Art."

Aarrrggghhh, come on, can't something go right today! Annoyed, I replied, "Kurt, I am working on a pallet that is stuck in the racks. Once I am finished with it, I will be right there."

After I was done talking on the radio, the stuck pallet made a *pop* sound—probably a piece of wood that was jamming it. The pallet came forward and was fixed. I then made my way over to where Kurt was, which was about two minutes down the warehouse. As I drove up to him, I saw him shaking his head. I had a feeling that this was not going to be good. I parked my forklift and came up to him.

"Art, I swear, this is how I found it," he said as I came past a wall of pallets and saw what he was looking at.

Three pallets of juice, over 150 cases, had fallen and were all over the floor. None of the bottles or cases broke open themselves, so everything could be restacked. But still, it was going to take someone an hour or more to get this fixed. All I could do was let out a sigh.

"Kurt, what is the time of your appointment on the truck that you are working on?" I asked. He handed me his paperwork. Kurt was working an outbound truck with an appointment at 5:00 a.m., so we were six hours behind schedule. Keeping him here to help me fix this would make it worse.

"Is this truck a live truck?" I asked, and he nodded. Of course, it was a live truck.

"I will fix it. Can you bring me three empty pallets to restack this stuff on?" I asked.

"Art, I can stay and help you if you want. I get paid by the hour," said Kurt.

"No, we're too far behind on the schedule. I mean, look, your truck has a 5:00 a.m. appointment. Get me those pallets, and I can fix these by myself. If anyone needs me, though, let them know where I am." And with that, I started rebuilding the pallets. Kurt got me the empty pallets, and I started restacking. When someone called out on the radio for something, Kurt or another senior operator would get it so that I could work on these pallets.

While fixing them, my phone started ringing. When I took it out, I saw that it was Mark. Oh, good, maybe he will come in early today. I could really use it.

"Hey, buddy, are you volunteering to come in for more over-time?" I asked jokingly.

"Art," he said with a serious tone, "I might be sick."

"Oh no, you and the wife get that stomach bug again?" I asked. A few weeks ago, he had a bug that gave him problems and had to call off work for a day.

"No, Art, my wife is showing symptoms of the virus. On the advice of her doctor, we are both self-quarantining until the results of her COVID-19 test come back," said Mark in a tone of voice I would hear from maybe a doctor or a lawyer, not my buddy Mark.

Oh no, he might be infected.

"Art, I swear to you that I keep our workstation clean. I spray it down at the end of every shift!"

"Mark, calm down. It's okay. I do that too. Get yourself better, and I hope everything with you and the missus is okay. Did you tell Big Boss yet?" I asked.

"No, I am going to call him next. I tried calling the office, but I didn't get an answer," he said.

"You're not going to get an answer. He sent me a text this morning saying that he was going to be off all week," I said.

"Oh my god, Art, I am so sorry. There is no one to help you or the dispatchers, is there?" he asked.

"Don't worry about that right now, Mark. Just get yourself better and let me know how the test results go. Be careful and safe, buddy," I said.

"Yeah, you too, man. I am going to call Big Boss now," he said and hung up.

I think that was when the reality of the situation hit me. There was no backup for me. I was it now, buddy! You know, all the training in the world can't prepare you for what the feeling is like. It was not too far of a stretch to admit that for the first time, I was scared—not scared that I would be fired or that I wouldn't have a job but scared knowing that if I didn't come in, then it could possibly be a fatal blow to the operations. We would have to stop at this rate. We were out of backup people.

I looked back at it now, and one of the only things that I think kept me going the most was my family. Every year, I made a video postcard to show the girls when they are older what life was like for them growing up so they'd get to relive being little and see what they were like from when they were babies. When both of my girls were born, Joyce and I left messages for their future selves. For both of my messages, I promised the girls that while Daddy was alive, I would do everything I could to keep the family together and safe. It was something that I was very prideful of. Right now, that was being tested to the max as the literal world around us changed abruptly and in ways that we never anticipated or planned for. I made the decision there not to fold and not to cave—to keep going forward and not stop moving, tackling each challenge as it came at me even if it had to be multiple challenges at the same time.

I went back to restacking my pallets. When I was finished, I had figured that it was the right time to contact Big Boss to see if there was any possibility we could get some help. *No* was the answer. I looked at my phone and just sighed again. I then decided to send Joyce a message about what happened. I then asked her to tell her mom to stay out of her downstairs area by the coal fire. I didn't want to expose her to anything in case I was exposed. Fortunately for me, she told me, "Okay." Thank God.

There were only so many hours in a day that I was allowed to stay to keep working. Every possible problem that I could get my hands on, I solved. Luckily, there were no returns that came in by the time I left, so I had a pretty clear conscience about not leaving anything unfinished. Of course, even if I had, it would be waiting for me in the morning.

On the way home, I called my mother-in-law to make sure that Joyce had given her the message.

Ring, ring, ring.
Ring, ring, ring.
Ring, ring, ring.
Come on, pick up the phone.
Ring, ring, ring.
Ring—hello!

"*Baaa*, hey, Momma Joyce," I said, slightly startled because my phone was connected with the Bluetooth to the truck and every speaker just screamed at me. *Let me go ahead and turn that volume down.*

"Hi, I am not downstairs," she said.

"Okay, good. You got the message?" I asked.

"Yeah, are you okay? Is everyone okay at work?" she asked.

"The guy I work with is fine. He isn't sick. It is his wife, so they are quarantining them both. I will come up and do your fireplace really quick, no chitchat, okay? We probably should do it like that until we hear back from him," I said.

"Okay, bye!" she said.

"Bye, Momma Joyce."

Momma Joyce's phone etiquette was so admirable. When she was finished talking with someone, no matter who it was, she would just end it with, "Okay, bye," even if it was right in the middle of a conversation. I was not necessarily saying that I was looking for a thank you, but whatever. It was fine.

I got to her house, quickly took care of her coal stove, and then went to my house and took care of ours. After I was done, I came up from the basement to the outside and went to go into the mudroom. I waved at Joyce, and she smiled and pointed at the bottle of hand sanitizer strapped to the deck. I showed her that I went over to it. I put some of it on my hands and rubbed it up and down my arms and on my face. She then opened the door to the house.

"So the guy you work with is sick? Are you feeling okay? Do you keep a clean workspace? You don't, do you? Be honest!" she said.

"Okay, so Mark is not sick. It is his wife, and he is doing this as a precaution. Yes, we do keep a clean workspace, and I feel fine," I replied as I entered the house.

"Then why do you come home filthy sometimes?" she asked.

"Because what do you think I use to clean everything? Me!" I said jokingly. That seemed to make her feel a little better.

"You wear your respirator, right?" she asked.

"Yep, I am doing everything humanly possible to keep safe. And no matter how much of me right now wants to hug and kiss you, I need to go take a shower. I am beat. Do you need anything before I go take one?" I asked.

"No, go take your shower, then the kids and I will talk to you. The kids right now are in Joyce's room, playing video games, so just go get cleaned up. I will work on dinner," she said.

"Joyce, you do realize how much I appreciate you doing dinner and taking care of the kids, don't you? Without you, this place would fall apart. I really cannot thank you enough for what you are doing," I said, really trying to convey how sincere I was because it was true. If she wasn't there or wasn't doing what she was doing, the situation for everyone would be so much worse.

"You better appreciate what I am doing, mister!" she said jok-ingly. "Come on, go get cleaned up before supper so you can spend some time with the kids."

"Joyce, have I had a chance to tell you today that I think you are the most beautiful woman in the world and that I love you?" I said.

"I love you too. Now for the last time, go get cleaned up before I smack your butt with this wooden spoon!" said Joyce.

"Oooh, is that a threat or a promise?" I asked.

"Arthur!" she replied.

Joyce's Journal

Tuesday, March 24, 2020

Breakfast—Daily conference of gov. NY. He is talking about plasma studies of people who have the antibody. 14–21 days apex higher and sooner than we thought. Must increase hospital capacity.

I saw a report that car industry will start making ventilators.

NY gov.—staff needed—retirees, anyone in health care will be needed as a reserve staff.

I am thinking end of next week, I will put in a grocery pickup order. These are troubling days, but grateful we are well off and prepared.

My brother in South Korea let me know they have over 8,000 infected people.

Today was Arthur's 16th straight day at work. He plans to take Sunday off.

1/3 of world's population on lockdown. President wants to open country by Easter, April 12. "Raring to go by Easter."

Chapter 13

Day 17: The Hardest Hump Day and the Thursday after It

March 25, 2020, Wednesday

Beep, beep, beep.

I slapped the stupid alarm clock silent. I leaned over to kiss Joyce, and instead of a forehead, in the darkness, I miscalculated and got a mouthful of hair. I kissed her hair, whatever. "I love you," I whispered to her before I left. It was Wednesday—hump day, the midway point through the week. After this, it would literally be three more days until I *finally* got a break. Until then, though, with no Big Boss or Mark, I was going to need to do something. I needed to get someone to give me a hand with what needed to be done.

I practiced on the ride into work what I was going to say during the preshift meeting. I wanted to convey that it was temporary but urgent that someone needed to help me. It didn't have to be hard or complicated. Even simply helping me lump pallets or learning some simple inventory stuff would be enough. There had to be someone on the shift looking to maybe expand their skill set and be a more valuable asset to the team, no?

I pulled into the parking lot and clocked in. The forklifts whizzed around me as I was going down the docks, still busy. Walking up to the office, I could see a mound of problems sitting in the stage, just waiting for me.

Oooh boy, here we go, I thought.

During the night, Mark got to these problems, and only when it was something he hasn't seen or doesn't understand did it get to me. But that was rare. I walked by the pile of partial pallets. My guess was that this stuff was either damaged or expired product picked ahead of time to an order but went beyond shelf life before the order shipped, and no one knew what to do. Or it was a problem from an inbound that no one knew how to fix, or something to that effect. All these problems did add up, and given our volume, if they weren't addressed as soon as possible, they would just turn into one giant pile.

I walked into the office, and almost immediately I heard, "Mark is sick?" asks Jim.

"First off, how did you know that?" I asked. No one was supposed to know that beyond me and Big Boss. Maybe some of the supervisors on the other shifts or other buildings, but not Jim.

"Last night, when Mark didn't show up, they had a problem, so someone called him. And he told them that he wasn't coming because he was being tested," replied Jim.

"Oh, for crying out loud, well, now you know," I said.

"So there is no Mark, just you? That's awesome. Well, here is a stack of problems from just me. They had stuff from the second shift too. They just put it on your desk," said Jim. "Oh, also, we got some more returns back. I didn't have any room in the dock doors, so I put them out in the yard."

I took what Jim had given me and got back to my desk. Boy, was there a lot of stuff. I sat down at my desk and yelled out to Jim, "Jim, keep the returns in the yard. I am not going to get to them today, and with Mark not here, they are just going to have to wait."

"All right. Just keep putting them in the yard?" he asked.

"Yeah, I will try to get to them as soon as I can. It will be easier on Saturday because Calieb will be here," I said with a resigned tone in my voice.

"That's a lot of stuff to put in the yard," said Jim.

"I know," I said. There really wasn't much else that I could do. There were too many problems that had built up from the previous shifts, not to mention all the new problems that I was going to face throughout the day. I really hoped that I could get someone from the shift to help me out.

I prepared for the preshift meeting and got everything ready. After letting everyone know how much work there was for today and getting volunteers for overtime for the next day, I then hit them with the request.

"Guys, as you know, we are working with a severely reduced staff. We are all stretched really thin, but I need to ask a question to everybody. I need to ask, is there anyone here willing to work with me and learn some basic inventory tasks so that it frees me up to help out other people? Simple stuff, returns or how to do damage, because I am getting hammered with it, and ultimately, if I could have someone help me, it would help us all go faster," I said as I scanned the group.

Crickets.

Absolute crickets were all I heard.

Not a single hand went up, and not a single person stepped forward. I was pretty much on my own in the inventory world at this point. Not exactly throwing up the surrender flag, I did want to make my feelings known to the group.

"Okay, team, I am not a supervisor, and I can't make you do something you don't want to do. However, I want to let each of you know that if you need help out on the floor, you call specifically for me, and I say that I cannot help you, that is not a lie. I cannot help you. I can assure you that there will be a very good reason behind it, but I won't provide you that reason. I will simply say I am unavailable to help. After that, you are on your own to solve the problem and deal with the consequences of it. Given everything going on in today's day and age, I guess this definitely would qualify as an end-of-the-world situation. Everyone, work safe," I said as I dismissed the meeting.

Jim came running up to me as I walked back into the office. "Two things. One, we have a return here."

"Oh, come on, I hope someone is getting a talking-to. This is ridiculous. We are in the middle of a pandemic, and they are sending us all this stuff back!" I yelled.

"Ummm, okay, well, that's great and all, but what do you want me to tell the truck driver?" asked Jim.

"Put it in the yard for now. I will get to it when I can," I replied. "What was the other thing?"

"Did you just tell everyone on the shift that it was the end of the world?" asked a shocked Jim.

"Of course, not," I said. "I said it's an end-of-the-world *situation*."

With that, we went back to doing all the busy work. I was able to work through all the problems from the previous shifts and then eventually got to ours. But by the time that happened, it was more than halfway through the day. Some tasks that were normal—every-day goals of the inventory team—I was just flat out abandoning. Anything that was mission-critical to moving everything forward was taking priority. I had to triage everything from nonessential to essential work and focus on everything that was going to stop the operations if I didn't fix it right then and there.

So how did I do that? The first thing I abandoned was freshness; ensuring that the oldest-dated product left the building first used to be a specialty of mine. At this point, though, juice was moving so fast that it probably didn't matter if I was paying attention to it or not. It was not like I had the time to anyway.

The next thing to be abandoned was cycle counts. That was where you had to count every location in the building. Normally, this was done every thirty days, though at this point, if it was done, great. If not, then oh well.

The list of things not getting done was, in my opinion, important, but it wasn't mission critical. If we shipped out of rotation or did not count a location, the trucks would still move. Anything that wasn't going to stop the operations would sit off to the side until I had a chance to get to them.

What did take priority were the problems that stopped us from either loading or unloading the trucks. Were the orders allocating right? Was anything dumped? Were the trailers closing correctly? Those were what I tried to focus on—as much as I could anyway.

While I was on the floor, fixing a problem, I heard over the radio, "Art, this is Kurt. Do you have a copy?"

Even though I was busy, I still felt that I might be able to walk him through any problems he might have. "This is Art. Go ahead."

"Art, I have a problem with my pallet. Do you have a second to look at it if I bring it to you?" he asked.

He was trying to solve the problem, and if all I had to do was look at the pallet, I had time for that.

"Yes, sure, bring it over to me."

A minute later, he brought over his problem. The pallet looked like it had fallen over and was rebuilt wrong.

"What do you think, Mr. Art? Can I ship this like that?"

I looked at it and, not seeing any damage, scanned it to see what it was. "Well, it's the correct item number and quantity, just the wrong stack pattern. The inventory part of me says, 'Don't ship it. Restack it.' The other part of me says, '*Ship it!*'"

"Which part of you are we going to listen to, then?" asked Kurt.

"Ship it. We don't have time to restack it a third time. If I get an email about it, I will take responsibility," I said.

Kurt looked shocked. "Are you sure, Artie?"

"No, not really, but as long as nothing is damaged or leaking, ship it," I replied as my heart sank because I really couldn't believe what I was saying.

Kurt said, "Okay," and off he went.

I know, I know. It was just a minor detail. The customer wasn't getting shorted, but I spent a career of being 100 percent correct all the time. And even being one speck off made me feel like I didn't do my job right. But for the time being, ship it!

By the time I had finished up fixing everything that was in front of me from my shift, my day was over. Anything else that was going to happen was going to have to wait for the next day. I swiped my card, and out the door I went.

It was a very nice day out but still chilly. I didn't know if the kids would have loved to be out in the cold, but there was a blue sky with lots of sun, which did take the edge off the chill. I couldn't wait to get home, though. What a day.

On my way home, I did notice a few more people than normal out walking their dogs or out for a jog, dressed up like a snowman.

Nowhere was this more prevalent than when I drove past Frances Slocum State Park. The park came along one side of Carverton Road, which was how I got home sometimes. Next to the road was the boat launch, but on the other side of the lake, you could see a walking trail that winded its way next to the shoreline. The park itself had dozens of nature trails that I sometimes took the kids on in the winter months because there were less critters out, but the one on the shoreline was very pretty. And even though we were supposed to be inside and limiting travel and social distancing, when I drove by the park, I couldn't believe it.

The parking lot was packed, and I mean packed. You would swear you were driving by the parking lot of a theme park or something. There were more people than I had ever seen at that park at one time. My guess was that there were a lot of people from the cities Wilkes-Barre and Scranton that were just getting cabin fever, which I understood, but the other side of the lake on the trail looked like a constantly moving conveyor belt of people—like those animal shows that showed you lines of ants moving from the colony to a piece of fruit. That was what it looked like. How could you possibly enjoy an afternoon walk in a nature forest if the entire time, your nose was up someone's rear and someone had their nose up yours? Unbelievable! *No thanks, you can have that COVID-19 party you want. I don't want any of it!*

When I got up to my mother-in-law's house to take care of her coal stove, she was nowhere near me again. After working on her coal stove, I yelled up the cellar steps to the upstairs of her house. Luckily, the door was open.

"Hey, Momma Joyce!" I yelled as loud as I possibly could.

"Whaaat! Are you here?" she said, and I heard her start to walk toward the cellar door.

"Don't walk to the door if you can hear me! I worked on your coal stove, and it's good. I will be up tomorrow," I yelled.

"Okay," she hollered back, "did you hear anything from your friend at work?"

"No," I barked back, "I have not heard anything. When I do, I will let you know. Just keep your distance from me for the time being."

"Okay," she yelled back down, and out the door I went.

I went down to our house and did my updated routine down there, being careful not to touch even the dogs as I made my way through the house to take a shower.

"Dad!" yelled Clara through the bathroom door as I was washing up.

"Yeah, hon?" I asked back.

"Joyce, um, Joyce won't give me back my doll. She stole it from me!" she yelled.

"Tell you what, sweetie, don't worry about it for now. But in eleven years, steal your sister's boyfriend as payback, okay, hun?" I yelled back.

There was a brief pause, but then she yelled back, "Okay." Then she ran off.

Boy, this parenting thing was easy if you knew what you were doing.

After my shower, I went downstairs to where Joyce and the kids were already eating. I sat down, and the first question that Joyce hit me with was "Why is Clara going to steal Joyce's boyfriend?"

"Not a clue, hon. Anyway, how was your day?" I asked, quickly trying to change the subject.

"Fine. I am working on a big grocery order again online and will try to pick it up next week like we had talked about before. Other than that, nothing new. How is your friend from work? Is he doing okay?" she asked.

"I haven't heard from him, so I am hoping he is doing okay," I said. I then looked at both kids, who were sitting at the table with us. "You kids were good for Mom today, right?"

"Yeah, they were good for me," said Joyce. "Hey, on Friday, if you are not going to be too late, the weather is going to be nice. Do you want to take the kids up to the park if there are not a lot of people?"

"Oh, let me tell you what I saw, Joyce, when I went by today. It was like people were moving on one of those belts you see at airports. The parking lot was nuts, and there were hundreds of people there," I said, recounting what I had seen earlier in the day.

"Seriously?" asked a surprised Joyce.

"Seriously, I have never seen that many people there in my life. I am guessing all the city folk are getting restless. I don't know about going to the park."

I didn't mean to crush the spirit of everyone in the room, but it looked like everyone had already talked about it before I got home. Joyce and the kids all had this sad look on their faces like, "Oh well, can't do that."

"But I'll tell you what we can do. Does everyone want to go up to the church parking lot and ride bikes?"

The kids' faces lit right back up.

"*Yeaaah, Mommy, can we please do that?*"

"Yeah, I don't have a problem with that," said Joyce.

"Most of the time, there aren't any cars there, especially since the virus. Every once in a while, there is someone there trying to grab a cell phone signal, but that's basically it. All right, as long as the weather holds out when I get home on Friday, that is what we will do," I said.

Everyone seemed to be a little happier with that plan. Joyce and I could sit and talk while the kids played, and we wouldn't have to worry about anyone else being there that we would have to socially distance from. It was something for the kids to look forward to, and although before all this, it would seem like something so mundane or uneventful or something not to get excited about, at this point in time, it meant the world to these kids.

Joyce's Journal

Wednesday, March 25, 2020

$2 trillion stimulus bill passes this morning. 53,221 cases, 700+ deaths in USA, 435, 006+ cases 19,600, deaths (worldwide).

I began a grocery list for things we will run out of in 30 days or have used up. I am going to try to do a store pickup order end of next week.

Day 18

March 26, 2020, Thursday

Beep, beep, beep.

I slapped the stupid alarm clock silent. I groggily got up, just barely able to move. I was tired and achy still. "I love you," I whispered to Joyce as I kissed her shoulder and got up to go to work.

"Two more days, Artie, two more days," I muttered to myself as I walked out of the bedroom. As long as I could make it until Saturday night, I would then finally a day off.

The ride into work was uneventful—a little bit of an increase in traffic but not much. The sign along the highways still flashed messages for everyone to still stay at home and limit travel. I wondered how long those signs were going to be up like that?

I got to work and clocked in. It looked like Calieb asked a few of the weekend-shift guys to come in early because there was only one forklift available for me to use, and was the crappy old one. It was a forklift, though, and I didn't protest too much as I got onto it. I meant, I did protest, but it was just to myself because frankly, at this point, no one else was going to listen.

The day started out pretty uneventfully. Everything was still busy, and everyone had to at least work one day during the weekend. But they got to choose. For the most part, everyone was choosing Saturday. We were making it work with the workforce we had, but a lot of people were like me: just tired, just looking for that one day of reprieve. And honestly, that day couldn't come soon enough.

Toward the end of the day, I was working on a pallet that had fallen over in front of a dock door. People were continuing to call out for me. And anyone with an issue that I could help with over the radio, I did, but I couldn't leave this pallet because it was blocking a congested travel lane. While I was trying to get that done, answering the radio calls, and avoiding getting run over, Wisecracker came up to me on his forklift.

"Yo, you busy?" he asked.

"No," I replied, "I am just taking my pet cases of product out for a walk. Why?"

"I was sent to a location, and a pallet in there fell over. This is where it is," he said as he showed me a piece of paper with a location.

"Do you need help picking it up, or did you pick it up and saw it had damage?" I asked.

"No, that's not my job. I just skipped over it, but I wanted to let you know," he replied.

Oooh, cool, he found one of my triggers. You see, there was a difference between someone saying, "I can't help because I don't have the ability to," and, "I don't feel that I am paid to do what you are asking me to do." Though, given that I was not really in a position to correct his action nor would any really be taken even if I did complain, I just brushed it off the best way I could.

"You know, I hope everyone who feels that way has a clean conscience for when they meet their maker," I said.

"What is that supposed to mean?" asked a surprised Wisecracker.

"You know exactly what it means. We're all paid the same for eight hours of work and overtime for right now, and instead of just picking up the few cases, people with that mentality just leave it for the next poor guy to fix instead of addressing it when they find it," I said.

Either he was shocked that I was angry or just disgusted with what I was saying. In any event, he took off to finish his truck. After I was done fixing my original problem, I went out to find his. Going to the location on the piece of paper that he gave me, I found it. Literally just a few cases had fallen off the pallet. I quickly fixed the problem then went on my way. It was that kind of stuff that just annoyed me because the collective attitude that everyone has like that makes a ton of work for one person when if everyone would just fix the little problems, things would go faster. A lot of hands make light work, you know?

I put in my hours, clocked out, and headed home. During the ride home, I debated sending Mark a message on social media or through text. I wondered how he was holding up. I didn't know where his mindset was at, and I didn't want to bother him and make him think that all I cared about was when he was coming back to work. I decided to let it go and maybe wait until tomorrow or Saturday to check in on him. I hoped he was okay.

I got home and made sure all the coal stoves were squared away, and then I headed into the house to decontaminate. After that, I got to spend time with my family. One more day over. Tomorrow, its Fri-yay!

Joyce's Journal

Thursday March 26, 2020

Breakfast—Joyce's principal does an all-call with pledge, etc. every school day. Our administration is going to try to do a faculty meeting tomorrow on the internet. I have my expectation that it will not go over well because many can only check email. No one needs the added pressure. I imagine some of my kids are now babysitting their own siblings and don't have time or energy to cyber school.

65,000+ cases in US, 940 deaths.

NYC hospitals overwhelmed.

Gonna pull a frozen turkey from the freezer today. It will be meat for the weekend.

Next week, last grocery trip I did was on March 11, 2020. Looking forward to placing an order online late next week. I do get stir-crazy but know I should stay calm—stay home—stay safe.

There is a cruise ship in South America that cannot find a place to port. The cruise lines shut down days ago? What in the world???

Chapter 14

Day 19: The Last Friday

March 27, 2020, Friday

Beep, beep, beep.

I slapped the stupid alarm clock silent. *It was Friyay!* Literally one more day until the weekend. Tomorrow could not come soon enough! I leaned over, kissed Joyce on the forehead, and whispered, "I love you," to her. I got up out of bed, and maybe with a little spring in my step, I headed out of the bedroom and got ready to go to work. Because even though this was the nineteenth day of work, tomorrow I technically volunteered, so this was the last day of mandated overtime in a row. It was a new personal streak for the off season because we had never worked this much in March before—ever.

While I was getting my coffee ready for work and quietly singing to myself, I walked by the calendar in the kitchen and stopped and noticed something that immediately made my heart sink and the bounce come right out of my step. Today was Friday, March 27, 2020, and I had almost completely forgot about something.

When the pandemic had started, all our vacation time had been suspended or canceled and throughout the throws of everything I forgot that sometime last year I had specifically requested this Friday off from work. It was going to be a special Friday. It was a day that I was only going to ever get to experience twice as a dad.

Today was the day for Clara's kindergarten registration for school. When the governor had shut down the schools, the day was

166

canceled, and I had this awful feeling in my gut because I had nearly forgotten about it. I was so caught up in everything I had not noticed that this was supposed to be Clara's special day. And she was robbed of it. Her and every kid in the district was robbed of it, and I doubt Clara even realized it. They hadn't scheduled a new date, and with this pandemic, I didn't know if they ever would. That made me sad. Really, it did. Peanut got to experience kindergarten registration and the thrill of going into a school for the first time. And Clara, well, Clara won't get to experience that. I wonder what else these kids weren't going to get to experience.

The ride into work was uneventful, and I was even more encouraged as I approach the building and noticed the number of trucks had gone down quite a bit from a week ago. My guess was that the hoarding was over, *or* the stores were now stocked to the point where they could handle the sudden increase in demand. Maybe there was a little light at the end of this tunnel that we had been going through for two-plus weeks.

I clocked in, and we were busy. Calieb was the first one to greet me in the office.

"Good news, Artie."

"The voluntary mandatory day for the weekend has been canceled?" I asked excitedly.

"No, that would be nice, though. Big Boss sent me a text saying that he will be in on Monday," said Calieb.

"*Yes!*" I screamed into the office. Finally, we would get some support at work. Wow, this really was a Fri-yay. But I didn't get my hopes up too quickly.

"You think he will be?" I asked Calieb.

"Yeah, I don't think that he is going to take any more time off," he replied.

"Well, that's good news. Hey, did we get any more returns to come in?" I asked.

"Yeah, I counted twelve. Are you going to be getting to those today by any chance?" asked Calieb.

"I was going to try to get to them tomorrow. Why?" I asked.

"We really need those trailers to put different loads on. Is there any way we can get them at least stripped to the dock and have them put away tomorrow?" he asked.

I pointed to the dock. "There is way too much stuff staged out here already. Ugh, okay, how many of them do you need?" I asked.

"Five, but if you can get us three, we might get some drivers come in with empties. If you could get us five, that would be great," he said.

"Jim, put three of these in the door right now. I will start working them after preshift," I said. "I will get at least these three done first thing. If I have more time, I will do more. But this means that I am not going to be able to get to these problems here. Is there anything you can do for me, Calieb?

"I will stay some more overtime to try to help you out," said Jim before Calieb had a chance to respond.

"You're the man!" I exclaimed as I went out to do the preshift meeting.

I did the meeting with Calieb, who counted to see who was going to be doing what day for their voluntary mandatory overtime. After that, I started working on the customer returns. I really wished that someone had volunteered to do this because it was not that super complicated to do. It was just time consuming and slow. It was like trying to sprint through a vat of molasses; no matter how much energy you put into trying to go through it faster, it just doesn't seem to help.

I was finishing up the first return of the three that I had set myself out to do when on my radio I heard, "Art, this is Jim. Do you copy?"

"Go ahead, Jim," I said.

"Art, is there a chance you can come to the office and talk to one of the schedulers at corporate?" he asked.

"Jim, I don't really know much about scheduling. You at the desk would know more about that, and why?" I asked.

"They want to know if they can add three truckloads of donations for today," he said.

Donation loads? Donation loads right now? Are you kidding me? Besides the fact that basically inventory took care of the donation loads, we did not have the dock doors let alone the man power to work on three live truckload donations. A truck load donation is basically a full trailer of donated product. Something that large would probably be going to a large food-bank distributor or something else as large.

"Jim, I don't know, man. Three full truckload donations? Who is it for? Where is it going?" I asked.

He paused and replied, "They are three full donation loads for pandemic relief to New York City."

I had to pause. There were probably *a lot* of people right now who had gone two weeks without working, so anyone doing day labor or something that gave them a daily paycheck had no money to buy food and had to rely on food pantries. The food pantries were already relying on a strained source of donations to fulfill the need they had *before* the pandemic. So what was I supposed to do, say no? "Sorry I had to work on customer returns. And there is no one here to help me, so no food for you"?

"How much time do I have to get them ready?" I asked.

"The first driver will be here in fifteen minutes," he replied.

"Jim, did I ever tell you about Grandpa Becker?" I said while chuckling a little bit.

"What?" Jim cried out.

"Grandpa Becker was on merchant marine ships in WWII. He had two sunk from under him by the enemy, but he still made it out alive. If Grandpa Becker could come out of that, I can handle three trucks of donations. When I finish this return, save the door for the next donation, and we will rotate them through this door. If I have time, I will stage the product. If not, I will just load them as they come," I said.

"Aren't you the only one who does the donations?" said Jim.

"Yeah, it's going to be a looong day, my friend," I replied.

As I got done with the returns, the first donation load showed up. It was not that I was the only one who could do this. It was just there was a different way in the system of doing a donation load, and there were very few people besides inventory who have been trained on how to do them. As soon as I agreed to do them, I knew I just added on an hour to my day. I just prayed that Joyce wouldn't be too angry with me. I knew this was taking away from my time with her and the kids.

By the time the day was done, I had only gotten to about a third of what I had planned on doing. But the donation loads got done, and the relief supplies were going to be on their way. When I looked at the clock, I knew I was in trouble. I was about an hour and a half later than I have been since I was mandated the extra hours. I was tired, sore, and beat. I was ready to go home.

I clocked out and got in my truck to head home. I was just looking forward to lying down on the floor if I had to. I didn't care. I didn't even care about dinner. I just wanted to lie down. One more day of work until a day to rest—I couldn't wait.

When I got home, I went to work on the coal stoves first. Then after I was done doing that, I went in to say hi to everyone and then just collapsed on the floor. When I saw the girls and Joyce all dressed up in jackets and hats, waiting for me in the living room, I knew those plans were going to change quickly. *Gasp!* We were supposed to take the kids up to the church to ride bikes, and it was a nice day out.

"Hi, Daddy! Can we go ride bikes at the church?" asked little Joyce gleefully.

"Yeah, Dad, can we go?" asked Clara.

"Well," I said, trying to hide my fatigue, "we did say if it was a nice day, we would go. Do you girls have to go to the bathroom or anything before we head up there?"

"No, the kids went to the bathroom, and we have been waiting here for a bit. What happened?" asked Joyce.

"I had a problem at work that I had to work on before I left. I will get the kids' bikes and put them in the truck. Come on, girls!" I said as I changed out of my work boots into my sneakers.

"Dad, can you get your bike too?" asked Clara.

I barely had the strength to stand. "No, hon," said Joyce. "Daddy and Mommy want to talk. We will watch you from the back of the truck."

Thank you, Joyce!

I got the kids' bikes into the back as Joyce got the kids into the truck. As we headed up to the church, the kids were carrying on about how they were excited about getting to go ride bikes. Joyce, seeing that I was tired, reached into her coat pocket and pulled out a little baggie with a sandwich.

"Here," said Joyce, "we had a bite to eat already, but I made you a peanut butter and jelly sandwich."

She handed me the sandwich, and I gratefully accepted it. How did she know?

"Thank you so much, hon. I appreciate this."

"You're welcome," she said as I pulled into the church parking lot. The church that we were members of had been shut down since the beginning of the pandemic. Before, I used to go every Sunday and bring the kids to Sunday school. Joyce would sometimes come and sometimes not come. I never really pushed her into coming since we weren't all there anyway. The Sunday school was run at the same time as service, and the kids got more out of that than just sitting there, twiddling their thumbs and bothering me and Joyce. But now, with it shut down, it was pretty desolate.

I got the kids' bikes out of the back, and they went riding around. Joyce and I sat on the tailgate and watched them.

"Pretty busy at work today, huh?" asked Joyce as I ate my sandwich.

"Yeah, but on the bright side, it has been slowing down," I replied.

"You don't have to work on Sunday, do you?" said Joyce.

"No, no, I am not working Sunday. That will be my day of rest, and I am telling you, Joyce, I have been looking forward to it for weeks. All I want to do is chill with you and the kids," I said.

"Good, that's what we want too," said Joyce as I saw that she was watching Clara riding around. "I didn't tell her, but today was supposed to be Clara's kindergarten registration day."

"I know. I saw it on the calendar, and I remember putting in the vacation day for it. It's terrible that it all got canceled. Did the school say if or when they are going to reschedule it?" I asked.

"No," said Joyce, "even if they do reschedule it, I don't think it's going to be anytime soon. This whole thing is awful because she is going to miss out on so much."

"Yeah, I know, sweetie, but it has to be like this to keep them safe," I said, pointing to both the girls.

"Oh, I know that. Believe me, I know that. I just want to give her as normal a childhood as I possibly can," she said.

"You will. No, you know what? We both will. I am sorry that I haven't been home as much I wanted to. I hope you don't resent me for it," I said.

"No," said Joyce, "you had to go for the past few weeks, and the kids will be fine. Do you think it will ever slow down to where it is supposed to be for you at work?"

"Yeah, it's starting to now. I think the hoarding has stopped and that everything is going to go back to normal. I mean, you know, the new normal," I said as I watched both kids. Just then, a township police car drove by. Joyce and I smiled and waved at the policeman, and he waved back.

"Boy, I tell you, they are out in force for some reason," said Joyce.

"Why do you say that?" I asked.

"That is like the third time today that I have seen a township cop go up and down this road," she said with a concerned tone in her voice. "I wonder if they are looking for someone."

I should probably tell her now what was up. "No, hon, they are just looking *out* for someone."

"What does that mean?" she asked.

"Back at the beginning of all this, I had asked Chief if his officers were out to just add an extra patrol on our street because of me working so much," I replied. "I am not saying you couldn't handle anything if something happened. I just thought it wouldn't hurt to ask for the police to have a greater presence in the neighborhood, you know, if anything got crazy while I was at work."

Joyce put her arms around me as we sat on the back of the truck. "Well, that explains why all of a sudden, I would see the police cruiser drive up the road more often. Thanks. I know that you don't think that I am weak or anything. The girls and I really are glad that you did that. It just shows that you love us."

The rest of the time we spent up there, Joyce and I just watched the kids play in the parking lot. When they both came up to us and told us that they were getting cold, we packed everything up and went home. It was starting to get dark anyway.

I took a quick shower as Joyce made dinner. We talked about what we wanted to do on Sunday—my first day off in three weeks. While there were other people at work who were there as much as possible and sucked up lots of overtime, most of them didn't have kids, so I guessed they had the energy to do it. I had never gotten this much overtime before, so this one day would be a nice reprieve for not only me but everyone. I was just *so* looking forward to it.

After dinner, it was late enough to start heading to bed. The kids had gotten up late that day, so they weren't that tired. So I made a deal with them. If they would go to bed, I would put them to sleep and lie on the floor so that Mom could some have some quiet time to herself. They both agreed to it.

I got their toothbrushes ready, and they put on some pajamas. Before we went upstairs, I made sure everyone said good night to Mom. She said good night to all of us, and I said, "Why are you saying good night to me? I will be back down after the kids fall asleep."

"Yeah, right!" she replied.

I got the kids tucked into bed and put on a movie for them to watch as I lay on the floor. As I started drifting in and out of consciousness, I could hear the girls giggling and talking. I was fine with it. I was going to be out in a few minutes anyway. Then someone had this great idea.

Bam!

My eyes were closed, but I could tell that someone had just jumped off the bed. With my eyes still closed, I called out, "Girls, who was that?"

"Clara," said Peanut.

"Clara, what are you doing?" I said, keeping my eyes closed and hoping that whatever was going on would end quickly.

"I want to jump off the bed, Daddy," said Clara.

"Clara, please, Daddy is very tired. Please stay on the bed and watch TV until you fall asleep, okay?" I asked.

"Okay, Daddy," said Clara as she climbed back onto the bed.

The next few minutes were a blur because I was drifting in and out of it. It wasn't too much longer until I heard *bam* a second time, only on the second time, whoever jumped came really close to jumping on my arm because I felt a little foot land next to my shirt.

I opened my eyes, and there standing over me was Clara.

"Hon," I pleaded, "Daddy is very tied. Please, please, *please* stop jumping off the bed and go to sleep, okay!" I said, grabbing her by the shoulders.

"Okay, Dad," said a smiling Clara. And once again, she scrambled back onto the bed. I debated heading into my and Joyce's bedroom but decided against it because I wanted to give Joyce as much alone time as I could. I didn't want anyone to bother her.

I lay back down and closed my eyes, and this time, I heard both of them running around in a circle on the bed. I was getting more annoyed by the second. I didn't know if what happened next was stress induced or out of fatigue, but it was definitely COVID-19 related.

"Clara, no, don't push!" was the last thing I heard. After that, all I felt was pain because someone fell right onto my lap, and the amount of pain was immense. As I sat right up with the sensations flowing through my body, my eyes were closed. I was wincing in pain. I did open them briefly enough to see Peanut's foot smack me in the face, knocking me back down on the floor as she scrambled to get back onto the bed. When she tried to get off me, her foot had caught my shirt and ripped it. At this point, I had it.

"*Come on, guys!*" I barked. "*All I ask of you two is to lie down on the bed and watch a movie, and you can't do that? Do you know what's going on out in the world right now? There is a lot, a lot of bad stuff happening out there right now, and the only thing between out there and you two are Mom and Dad. Please, please, please just lie down and go to sleep!*"

As I got up, went to leave, and go get a new shirt, I heard both girls start to cry. I closed the door behind me and walked down the hall, trying to make it so that Joyce wouldn't hear what was going on. I went down the hall to my dresser to get another shirt, and while I was standing with my back to the hallway, I heard someone go running by me, heading toward the girls' room. Before they got there, they turned around and came to the doorway where I was still trying to put on my shirt.

I turned around while putting my new shirt on and was a little surprised to see Joyce there. The look in her eyes was not of anger but of disappointment and anguish. What had I just done?

"You know, their world changed too," said Joyce. Now her voice was getting louder. "Joyce, our little social butterfly, doesn't get to see her friends anymore. Clara may never get to go to her kindergarten registration. Both of them may never get to go to dance class or Sunday school for a long, long time. They sit in here all day because they don't want to go outside because it's too cold. When they aren't arguing with each other or fighting while playing video games, they are constantly asking me, 'When is Daddy coming home?' because they want to be with you."

Well, my now my heart just dropped.

"Sometimes I don't know what to tell them about when their dad is coming home because you have to be the one to save the world. Would it kill you to message me if you're going to be later than you expected so we won't be sitting in the living room with me saying to them every five seconds, 'Daddy will be home in any second, don't worry'? You have a family at home too, Arthur. Don't forget about us," said Joyce as she turned around and went to go down the hallway.

"Joyce, I will put the kids to bed, don't worry," I said as I started walking up behind her.

"No, you go to bed. I will try to fix this," said Joyce as she pointed for me to turn around.

And that was how the night ended for everyone. Instead of going into our bedroom and lying down, I didn't know why, but I headed for the couch in the living room downstairs. I grabbed my change of clothes for the next day and my alarm clock and went downstairs. I laid my head down, and that was the last thing I remember from that day. This sucked.

Joyce's Journal

Friday, March 27, 2020

19th straight day of Arthur working. Today would have been Clara's kindergarten registration.

Online faculty meeting today. I am just about at the point where I don't want to see what the numbers are for our country because it is overwhelming.

British PM Boris?? Has coronavirus. TGIF—weekend is tomorrow.

No school work for kiddo.

Kids watching TV. Math for Clara!!

Turkey is thawing for weekend. We have gravy, mashed potatoes, corn, and we will bake cookies or something similar.

Kids rode bikes up at church. Art and I sat on back of truck, it was very nice.

Chapter 15

The End of the Book, Not the End of the Story

March 28, 2020, Saturday

Beep, beep, beep.

I rolled over on the couch and just stared at the alarm clock. Why was I not motivated today to hit that thing? It just screamed and screamed at me to wake up. Yet I just stared at it. It went off for a few more brief moments before I finally did muster the strength to turn it off and get up to the start the day.

I sat up on the couch, no Joyce to kiss or to say I love you to. I was not feeling very good. It wasn't "the Rona." It was just me realizing how much of an idiot I was to my family. It was very lonely and dark in the living room. I knew I had to make it up to them, but not at 3:30 a.m. I got dressed, made my coffee, and made my way to work. The rest of the world might need me right now, but there were two little girls and the most beautiful woman I've ever known that needed me right now too.

I'll be 100 percent honest. I didn't really pay attention to anything on my drive into work that morning. The only thing I concentrated on was how much I really, really, *really* did not want to be going to work right now. I just had to figure out what I could do for the kids and Joyce. They didn't deserve that last night. They were only kids.

I clocked in, and for the amount of people that had volunteered to come in today, the parking lot was not as full as it should've been. When I went to clock in, there were forklifts available for me to use too. I was pretty sure of what had happened.

"Hey, good morning, Calieb," I said as I walked into the office.

"Wow, you came in. That's good," said Calieb.

Puzzled, I asked, "Why would you say that? Did you have a lot of people call off?"

"No, they canceled the mandatory overtime for anyone who didn't volunteer. I figured that you would have asked to not come in if that was the case," he said.

I just rubbed my forehead like I had a headache. *Are you serious!*

"When did they decide to do that?" I asked.

"Right after you left, the second shift got a call from Big Boss," said Calieb.

"Wow, that was nice. How come no one told me or called me?" I asked.

"You didn't pick up your cell phone?" he said.

"Oh, for crying out loud, I don't have cell phone service where I live, and… You know what, whatever. It's whatever. It is what it is." Boy, I was frustrated.

"Do you want to go home now?" asked Calieb.

"No, I just drove an hour to come to work. I'm not going to drive an hour back home with nothing to show for driving two hours this morning. Are we busy? Do I have time to get to the customer returns?" I asked.

"Actually, there is one here at the window right now," said Calieb as he pointed to a driver waiting in line at the dispatch window. He handed me the driver's paperwork, and I looked it over.

As the driver stood in the window, I yelled out, "Hey, buddy, is this you?"

"Yeah, why?" asked the driver.

"Why are they sending back all these orders? Aren't they running out of stuff on the store shelves?" I asked, wondering why, if everyone was hoarding supplies, on earth they were sending this stuff back.

"The distribution center these are all coming from closed down. I heard rumors that they have an outbreak of that virus going on in there," he replied.

Calieb and I just looked at each other. Holy crap, this virus was real and was having real consequences! I now felt even more of a jerk for cursing about these returns. They weren't sending them back because someone messed up on ordering. This driver was telling me that it was because the distribution center for the stores was shut down. Ugh, I was batting a thousand today, I tell you.

I told Calieb to put the driver into a door and that I would immediately start working him. While I was doing that one, I also told him that if he had the available dock doors, to put in all the customer returns he had in the yard into two other doors and that I would spend all day rotating through them. Calieb obliged and started doing what I had asked.

That was what I worked on for most of the day. Ironically enough, while working one of the returns, I recognized that I had done it as an outbound. This customer return was a truck that I had personally loaded when we had shipped it out the week before. It was nice to see that the load rode so well to the customer and back. It sort of made me a little prideful of my work. Too bad I was the only one who saw it, though.

I put in my hours and punched out. On the ride home, I was just playing out all kinds of scenarios of what I would do or what I would say. I just had to say or do something to say that I was sorry, but what? I couldn't stop and buy the kids a toy; Joyce would be upset that I went to the store. It was the end of winter, so there were no flowers to bring back. Maybe I could stop by one of the neighbor's—the one who owned horses—and actually buy a pony. I don't know, something.

I didn't even go up to my mother-in-law's to work on her coal stove. I just wanted to get home and do something, anything. I got out of my truck and walked up to the house. I could smell Joyce's cooking. She had made dinner. It smelled awesome, as it always did. What was I going to do?

I opened the door to the mudroom. The dogs were not in there, but I could see through the window to the kitchen that everyone was seated at the dinner table, eating. Joyce was looking at her plate, Peanut had her back to me, and Clara was taking a drink out of a cup.

What do I do? What do I say? Will they accept anything I even offer out there?

I held my breath, turned the knob, and opened the door to the kitchen. Both the kids turned their heads and looked at me. They looked scared, like I wanted to yell at them or something. It was heartbreaking. Joyce, well, Joyce had a poker face on. I couldn't even read her at this point. I thought, *Well, now's the time to do anything if you want to do something and fix this, big man.*

I went up to the kids, grabbed both their chairs, pulled them toward me, and began giving them a big hug.

"I am so sorry that I yelled at you girls yesterday," I said as I hugged them. "I am so, so sorry."

Both the girls reached up their hands and hugged me back.

"It's okay, Daddy," said Clara. "I'm sorry that I was running on the bed."

"Yeah, I am sorry too, Dad," said Peanut. "I didn't mean to fall on where you had your surgery."

At this point, Joyce got up from her seat, came over, and started hugging everyone too. "Okay, is everyone all sorry toward each other? Does everyone accept everyone's apologies?"

"Yesss," we all said in unison.

That feeling felt so good. We were able to move past it.

"But I wouldn't have fallen on Daddy if Clara didn't push me," said little Joyce.

"*I didn't push you, Joyce. You fell!*" insisted Clara.

"It's fine. Everything is fine. We all said our sorrys, and we all accepted them, right?" said Joyce.

"Yes," we all said again in unison.

The kids continued eating while I grabbed a plate and sat down with them. Joyce and I were talking about the day's events. She told me we were on some sort of lockdown orders. I don't know. She was happy to hear that Big Boss was going to be back in the office on Monday. In the meantime, while we were talking, the kids had both finished their dinners. Clara put her plate of whatever she didn't finish up on the counter. She then walked out of the room and went upstairs. Little Joyce was fiddling with something on her plate.

Joyce and I didn't really pay attention to what she was doing, but out of the corner of my eye, I saw that Peanut was breaking apart a soft pretzel that she had been given for dinner. I didn't even know we had any of those left. Joyce must have found them in the freezer! Anyway, she broke apart her soft pretzel into three equal parts. She then walked around the table, gave a piece to her mom, and then handed a piece to me.

"Oh, sweetie, I am okay you eat it. I didn't even know we had any of those left. I have not seen them for a long time," I said, trying to hand her back the piece that she had broken off for me.

"No, it's okay, Dad. When Mom was making dinner, she told us that these were the last soft pretzels we had and that she didn't know when we were ever going to get more. So I want you and Mom to have a piece of the last one," said Peanut with a tone of humbleness.

Joyce and I just couldn't believe what we were hearing. Here was our innocent daughter being so selfless, sharing what she thought could be the last three pieces of soft pretzel we would ever have. Joyce got up from her chair and gave Peanut a hug. I joined them.

I started to hear Joyce softly cry, "She's only eight years old," as she let loose from her hug and looked right at me. "She's only eight years old, Arthur, and she wants to share with us her last pretzel. She shouldn't have to do this."

I let go of Peanut and gave a Joyce a hug. "I know, hon. I know," I said as I rubbed her back.

"Do you guys not want the pretzel?" asked little Joyce with a confused look.

We all sat back down on our seats and ate the pieces of pretzel that were broken up for us. While we were eating the pretzel, Peanut got up to get herself a drink…of chocolate milk. This kid loved chocolate milk. I swear, her blood was 2 percent chocolate milk.

"Hon, do you think chocolate milk and all those soft pretzels go well together?" I asked her.

"I don't know. I think it's fine," replied Peanut.

"It's okay, Art. Let her have all the chocolate milk she wants. Pandemic!" said Joyce.

We all kind of chuckled.

"Hey, 'Nut," I said as she was finishing the chocolate milk, "do you think you can go upstairs and play video games with your sister for a little while? I want to hang out with Mom in the living room."

"Yeah, sure, Dad," said Joyce as she put the empty milk container in the trash.

She went upstairs as I started cleaning up after dinner.

Joyce helped put away stuff with me, and when we were done, she said, "So you want to hang out with Mom, do you?"

"Yeah, Mom is pretty cool," I said as I grabbed a bottle of moisturizing cream. "Want a foot rub?"

"Oh, I won't say no to a foot rub. I haven't gotten one of these in a while!" she said.

"I know. I have been slacking. Can't imagine why, though," I replied.

Joyce sat down on her chair, and I began moisturizing her feet. We talked and watched TV, and I gave her a foot rub. We did this for about twenty minutes until we could hear some commotion from upstairs.

"Don't worry about it. It's fine," I said. "Just let all the stress and tension come out to me through your feet."

"Mmm-hhmmm," said Joyce, enjoying it.

"*Get a bucket,*" I heard one of the kids yell. "*No, don't use my bucket. It will smell.*"

It was Clara yelling. Why was Clara yelling?

"It's fine, hon," I said, trying to delay the inevitable for as long as possible.

Then we heard both kids screaming.

"*Mooom,* Joyce threw up on herself!" we heard Clara bellow down to us from upstairs.

Seriously? I looked up from Joyce's feet and saw this deflated look on her face. "Sigh," Joyce said quietly to herself.

"I got it, hon," I said as I got up from the foot rub. "I will be back as soon as I can."

"Please come back!" said Joyce.

I put the cream away and headed upstairs. "I'm coming!" I yelled out to them.

I got upstairs and found Joyce on the floor of her room, sitting with a puddle of thrown-up chocolate milk in her shirt, which she was holding above her legs. *Awww, poor kid.*

"You okay, sweetie?" I asked as I helped her take her shirt off, being careful not to let any of the stuff come out.

"Dad, I don't feel so good. Can I take a shower?" she asked.

What was I supposed to do, say no?

"Sure, hon. I will start it for you, then you can go in and take your shower," I said as I took the shirt into the bathroom. I emptied its contents into the toilet and washed out what I could in the sink. I then put it in my laundry basket to do later and started a shower for her. I got the water at the right temperature, stepped out of the bathroom, and called for her to take her shower. She went in and took her shower while I stayed outside the bathroom in case she needed anything.

"You guys okay up there?" Joyce yelled up to us.

"We're okay. Joyce threw up into her shirt. Nothing got on the floor. We're good," I said back.

As I stood outside the bathroom, Peanut called out to me, "Dad, I am done."

"Do you have a towel on?" I asked.

"Yes," she said, and I went in to help her dry off and comb her hair. I had been combing the kids' hair since they were babies, and it was usually after I was done giving them baths. We talked, and I gently tried to get all the knots out of her hair. She *hated* when I combed her hair because she said that I was too rough, but I didn't think I was. I've always thought these kids tried to eat their hair way too much. While I continued brushing, we heard wife Joyce yell up to us.

"Did you guys just flush the toilet or something up there?" asked Joyce from down in the living room.

Little Joyce and I just kind of looked at each other, puzzled.

"Ummm, no, why?" I asked.

"Why do I hear running water, then?" replied Joyce.

Peanut saw my eyes get really big really quick.

"Hon, stay here," I said as I jumped up. Joyce's chair downstairs in the living room was next to the vent for the coal furnace, so while it was very warm there in the winter because of the coal furnace, she also could hear anything that might be going on downstairs come up through register. Directly underneath where Joyce's chair was where the waterline from the well came in. Living in the country, we didn't have city water but rather a well pump that gave us the water we needed. If she was hearing running water, there was only one thing that I could think of that would cause that.

I ran down the stairs, and as I headed into the living room, I could see steam coming up from the vent.

"*Oh no!*" I screamed out.

Joyce was sitting in her chair and hadn't noticed the steam coming up. When she heard me yell, she looked over and said, "What is that?"

I ran past her down to the basement where I could see what happened. There was a break in the waterline to the house. It was now pumping water directly onto the coal stove.

"*Oooh no!*" she could hear me yell.

I saw where the break in the line was. The waterline came in from the wall and to a T-junction pipe. From there, the water went into one pipe into the pressure tank for the house or to an old pipe for a koi pond that used to be on the outside of the house years and years ago. There was no shut-off for the water pipes until after the T-junction. I could not isolate the break.

"*What happened!*" yelled down Joyce.

"*The waterline going out to the old coy pond broke. The coal stove is now getting soaked!*" I yelled back.

"*Can you shut off the water before the break?*" asked Joyce.

"No, there is no shut-off until after the break. I am going to have to turn of the well," I yelled up.

Quickly I unplugged the coal stove so the steam would stop and wouldn't short out. But that meant the fire would be out, and I didn't have anything to start it back up again. I then turned off the breaker for the well pump. While the pump was off, it still took about five minutes for the system to completely drain out. The entire time, it was wet, damp, and almost like a sauna downstairs. Unfortunately, now, with the pump off and everything in the system drained, there was no water for the house. I inspected where the pipe had broken and saw that I did have the tool to fix it but needed to go to a hardware store or plumbing supply store to get a cap to close off the pipe. You had to be kidding me right now.

I came upstairs to the living room, but Joyce wasn't there. I went into my shop to get my plumbing bag, and when I came back into the living room, I heard someone. I heard wife Joyce talking to a crying Peanut at the top of the stairs. I went running up to where they were. Peanut was still sopping wet with Joyce leaning over, hugging her.

"You okay, Peanut?" I asked.

With tears coming from her eyes, she looked up and said, "Dad, we don't have any water anymore?"

"Oh, sweetie, it's okay. Daddy can fix it," I said.

"You can?" she asked.

"Yes, Daddy can fix it. See, I have my plumbing bag full of tools. I just have to turn off the water for a few hours. Everything will be okay," I said, giving her a big hug. "Now why don't you go get changed, okay?"

She seemed to brighten up a little bit. "Okay, thanks, Dad."

"How bad is it?" asked Joyce.

"Well, the waterline that used to go out to that old koi pond broke, but there is no shut-off. Luckily, where it broke, I can fix it with a cap, but I don't have one. I am going to need to go tomorrow morning first thing to a hardware store to get the part," I said.

"What about the coal fire?" she asked.

"I unplugged it because I didn't want the motor to short out, and I also wanted to stop the steam. But now the fire is out, and I am out of anything to start it with," I said.

"The weather isn't going below freezing tonight, so the pipes won't freeze. It will be okay. We will just turn on the baseboard heaters," said Joyce. "You need to get changed now, wet boy."

I was soaked from head to toe, but I still needed to do Momma Joyce's coal fire. I dropped off my plumbing bag down in the basement before I left. While Joyce kept the girls occupied, I headed up to my mother-in-law's to work on her coal fire. I walked in the upstairs door, cold, dripping wet, and just exhausted. Momma Joyce was sitting on her couch, doing some sort of work with fabric. I knew I was trying to keep my distance from her. I was in a rush, but she was more than six feet from me. So I guess we were both okay.

"A little cold to be out swimming, isn't it, Arthur?" asked Momma Joyce.

"Waterline in the house broke. I just got done wrestling with it," I said.

"Oh no, well, can you fix it?" she asked.

"Yeah, I can fix it. I have the tools. I just have to go to the hardware store tomorrow morning to get the parts," I said.

"Oh, okay. Well, that's good," she replied.

"It's just getting tough, though, you know. I finally get one day off, and now I have to deal with this," I said, kind of defeated.

"Arthur, I was born during World War II, and my husband fought in Korea. Is anyone going to be shooting at you while you are trying to fix the pipe?" asked Momma Joyce.

"No," I sheepishly replied.

"Then you will be fine," she said, smiling.

"Thanks, Momma Joyce. I am going to take care of your coal fire and head out. Do you need anything else?" I asked.

"No, thank you for taking care of the fire for me," she said.

"No problem," I said as I headed to her coal stove. I worked on that and then went home when I was done. Joyce got the kids to go to sleep while I changed into something drier. She walked into the bedroom as I was setting my alarm clock to wake me up in time to be the first person at the hardware store.

"Thanks for putting the kids to sleep again, hon. I appreciate it," I said as I climbed onto my side of the bed.

"Yeah, you have a good excuse tonight. You set your alarm clock to be the first person at the store?" she asked.

"Yeah, I got my respirator and even some blue rubber gloves to wear. I will be safe while in the store," I said, getting under the covers. "You want to cuddle?" I asked, opening out my arm for her to hug me.

She got into bed. "I know you will be safe. I just hope I can take my shower in the morning."

"You will be able to take your shower only if I get to come in there with you!" I said, laughing.

"Yeah, right, you wish!" she said as we settled in to watch some TV. "Weather looks like it's going to rain tomorrow. Just get down there first thing."

"You got it, boss lady," I said. We both watched TV for as long as we could—well, as long as I could at least. I fell asleep first. I was pretty sure of that.

Joyce's Journal

Saturday, March 28, 2020

NY gov. mouth ventilators NY bought— training 3,000 national guard on manual ventilators. 24-hr. care. "No thank you," we need ventilators!

Read last night the workers for the company that does the online grocery shoppers may go on strike. UGGGGHHH! Sure, my order is scheduled for tomorrow!

Monday when they may go on strike. We still have plenty of provisions, though. Lots still in pantry. Turkey dinner tomorrow.

102,920+ cases, 1,590 deaths in USA. So much about the "15 cases that would drop to zero," as president said weeks ago. Apex 14–21 days (height). USA has the most reported cases of any country.

Global 621,636 cases, 28,658 deaths.

I hope some immunotherapies or drugs come on the market soon. Luzerne, Pike, and Wayne Counties now on stay-at-home orders.

March 29, 2020, Sunday

Beep, beep, beep.

I quickly slapped that alarm clock off. This was supposed to be not only my day off but Joyce's day off too. She woke up every time I woke up with that stupid alarm clock. I got up quickly and got changed to go out. I looked out the window, and it was not raining yet. Not that the rain affected anything inside the house, but I didn't want the filters on my mask getting wet because they were made of paper. And I didn't have any replacement cartridges. I couldn't imagine trying to find new ones right now.

I thought about the places closest to where we were in Harding that might have what I needed. I took a chance and picked the hardware store down in West Pittston. If they didn't have it, then someone downtown should have something. As long as I stayed away from the bigger chain hardware stores, I should be okay—less people and less traffic. I got in my truck with my masks and rubber gloves, and away I went. As I drove, I noticed that the weather conditions were getting dark and moist outside. It was going to rain and rain very hard very soon.

I got down to the store, and I was in luck. I actually was the first person at the store! I parked and went up to the doors. I had to wait a minute because they were still locked as I got there just at opening time. After a few brief moments, I did see someone in the store heading to the doors. I also saw them pause as they looked at me like I was someone that was nuts, standing at the door with a gas mask. A young lady came up to unlock the doors.

"Good morning," she said with a concerned tone in her voice. "Early bird gets the worm, huh?"

As she said that, a bolt of lightning flashed close behind the building, and the thunder cracked through the air, startling us both.

"Oh, wow, thunder and lightning in March? How often do you see that," she said as I went into the store.

"Not often, I guess. Hey, I need these parts to fix a plumbing problem at my house. Can you help me?" I asked as I showed her what I needed.

She walked with me back toward the plumbing supplies, and I got what I needed. After that, she rang up my purchases and bagged them up. I paid for my purchases, and as I was heading out the door, I heard my phone go *ding*. I looked at it and saw it was a message from Mark. He and his wife had tested negative, and he would be back to work on Monday. Both Big Boss and Mark would be back on Monday. I guessed things really were starting to turn around.

I got in my truck to leave, and it started raining. Lightly at first, but it picked up more and more as I headed home. By the time I pulled into the driveway, I could barely see the road in front of me. But I didn't care about that too much because I was finally home.

I jumped out of the truck and bolted toward the basement stairs. I didn't want to wake everyone in the house because it was still sort of early. My plumbing bag was already there, so the fix took me only a few minutes. After I was done, I turned on the breaker to the well pump. If this didn't work, I was going to get soaked all over again. The well pump kicked on, and the cap at the end of the threaded pipe held with no problem. The crisis was over. My one thing that I had to do today was done. *Finally, now I could relax!*

I cleaned up the work area and brought my plumbing bag back up to my shop. After I put all that away, I went upstairs to tell Joyce that the water was back on and that everything was okay now. As I climbed the stairs, I saw Joyce staring out a window in the hallway.

"Hey, good morning, beautiful. The break is all fixed, and the water is back on. If you hear hissing or anything from the shower or faucet, it is because there is air in the waterlines. It will go away," I said as I went to give her a hug.

"Thanks, Artie. How much do you love me?" she asked.

"That's a loaded question. I don't know. How about thiiisss much!" I said as I gave a really tight bear hug.

She gave me a kiss on the cheek and giggled. "No, silly, like, how much."

"I don't know, lots. Why?" I asked.

She pointed out the window where we could both see that a rain gutter was clogged, the pouring rainwater overflowing out of the side where it was forming a large puddle on the ground next to the foundation. When that happened, the rainwater seeped through the original rock wall foundation and flowed into the basement. The best part was, where the clog was located was right next to where the power lines came into the house. I had to reach around the power lines into the metal gutters during a thunderstorm to unclog the drain. Ugh, seriously? I had two options: either play dumb, pretend like I didn't know what she was talking about, and just let the water flood our basement or suck it up and fix it. How could I say no to such a beautiful smile?

"I see it. I will get it," I said as I released my grip from her.

"Thanks, hon. Do you want to use the roof above the mud-room?" she asked.

This would be the fastest and easiest way out there because there was a window from the upstairs bathroom that overlooked the roof of the mudroom. Crawling in and out of that window was a pain, though.

"I will help you out the window."

"Yeah, that's the fastest way to get out there, I reckon," I said. We both went into the bathroom, and I took off my pants and socks while Joyce opened up the window.

"Whoa!" cried Joyce as the wind and water whipped in through the opening.

"Okay, when I get out there, just shut the window behind me so you don't get yourself and the floor all wet, okay?" I said.

"Yeah, no problem. Are you sure you want to go on the roof in your underwear and T-shirt?" asked Joyce.

"Yeah, why not? If I get hurt, the guys at the fire department will have a funny story to tell for years. 'Hey, remember when old man Becker fell off his roof because he tried to unclog a drain during a lightning storm in his underwear?' I will be a legend in this town," I said, laughing.

Joyce laughed too. "Okay, come on. Get going. There is water all over the bathroom floor."

I climbed out the window in the pouring rain. It was wet *and* super cold—awesome! It was pointless to try to rush this stupid job because I was already soaking wet, so I took my time as I stood up on the roof. I got up, slowly walked over to where the clog was in the rain gutter, carefully put my arm up, and started feeling around in the gutter for the clog. At the same time, I had to keep my eye on the power lines, which were rocking slowly back in forth in the rainy wind. How did this thing get clogged anyway? There were no trees this high.

I felt where the downspout was and immediately could sense a lot of wet leaves clogging the drain. I started pulling them out and throwing them down onto the ground below. The more I got out the more pressure built up to go down, and *glug*. The drain was unclogged! All right, finally!

I gave Joyce a thumbs-up to open the window, and she pointed to the end of roof of the mudroom. There was a second gutter that was also apparently clogged. Through the rain and the fog of the window, she must have seen my head drop down in resignation because when I looked back up, she was smiling and gave me a thumbs-up. I nodded my head. *What's one more gutter to unclog?* I thought.

The problem was the roof was either softer than I had expected, or I was heavier than I had expected. Either way, I did not like the feel of the roof as I walked toward the other gutter. The pitch was shallow. It was not a steep, monstrous roof, so I wasn't worried when I got on all fours…in my underwear and a T-shirt…in a thunderstorm…and crawled my way toward the next and hopefully *last* gutter that I was going to have to unclog. The further I went, the softer the roof felt, so by the time I was at the gutter, I was on my belly, crawling my way down.

Through the pouring rain, which by now was making it hard for me to see because the water was just streaming into my eyes, I found the gutter and started feeling around. I felt the clog and started to tear out the leaves that were clogging this one too. I kept pulling until I heard the *glug* that I was waiting for. After I heard that, the water immediately started draining properly. *Yes!*

I turned myself around and started crawling up the gritty, wet, cold, miserable roof until I got to a point at which it was stable enough to support my weight. I stood up and walked up to the window. I tried to lift it open. It was locked—ugh! This time I gave two thumbs-up and the most innocent puppy-dog smile I could muster to try to get her to open it up and let me in. By this time, though, it was too foggy on the glass, and the rain pouring down was so hard that I couldn't see if she saw my pleas to let me in. Finally, after what seemed like an eternity, I heard the window unlatch and open. I jumped through the window and scrambled in. I was a wet, soggy heap on the bathroom floor.

"Oh my god, I am so sorry! I didn't know how it locked!" said Joyce.

My eyes were still full of water, so I couldn't see too well as I got up and turned around to close the window. "That's okay, hon," I said as the window was shut. "There isn't a problem that we can't solve together, right?"

"We got this, Artie," said Joyce with a smile.

*****

And this is where this book ends. But I can assure everyone that this is not where the story ends. As of the time I am finishing up these last few paragraphs, Joyce, the kids, the dogs, and now a cat *and* yours truly are all doing okay.

When the pandemic first hit, I think it made me realize just how much I truly took for granted in my life. Not saying I wasn't appreciative of what I had, but the world moved sooo quickly that little things would get over looked. Joyce and I both worked, and when we weren't working, we were wrapped up in a hundred other things that made stuff like spoiled food in the fridge seem like it wasn't a big deal because why? We could just go to the grocery store and get more. More—there was always going to be more. Because why not? There was always stuff before. There is stuff now. There will be stuff in the future. The idea that we would have food shortages or rationing in the stores was just something we have never been exposed to.

But that has changed now. Now we don't waste in our house; everything gets used, eaten, or whatever. We appreciate the little things more, I think. I remember when we were deciding on whether or not to have a second baby and were like, "Well, we should so they can have someone to play with at home." But now it's like, "Thank goodness Joyce and Clara have each other through all of this." So what was the motivator behind me writing this book?

We all face what seems to be like insurmountable obstacles in our lives. Through my own lifetime, there have been very few goals that I was not able to meet—maybe one or two, and what they were, well, that's a different book altogether. But the point is I kept going. Just because you have a goal and don't achieve it doesn't mean it will end you.

My goals before the pandemic were pretty simple: go to work, get paid, pay bills, work on the coal stoves, take the kids to dance, keep everything the same, yadda, yadda, yadda. But the pandemic changed that. Now it's this: keep the kids safe, keep the family safe, do whatever I need to do to make sure we are all okay.

You need to keep going. Joyce, wife Joyce, always says that there is a reason for everything. And there is a reason for this. There is a reason for what is going on right now. I don't know what that could possibly be, and maybe I will never know what the reason is. But you need to keep going.

And then it's "Why? Why do all of this? Why keep the kids safe? Why keep the family safe? What does it matter if I don't reach these goals?" Well, it matters to my kids that they are safe. It matters to my wife that we are safe. It matters to me that we are safe. They are everything to me. When I was a young man, I used to pray all the time for God to send someone to me that I could love, take care of, and have a family with so that there could be more love. I guess also that there was someone that remembered me and remembered that I mattered to them. After waiting for what seemed like a long time, I did find someone who loved me. I was blessed with my best friend, who I am proud to call my wife. I am blessed with two beautiful kids who are healthy and for the most part love me. That is why I keep going. I got what I wanted, and I have to keep it for as long as I possibly can, right up until the day that I end up at the big inventory desk in the sky.

If you're reading this book, I hope you have someone special too and that you appreciate and take care of them too. It doesn't have to be a wife, a girlfriend, or a fiancé. It could just be a friend. Be nice and appreciate them, especially now. Don't you feel good when you are treated nicely and are appreciated?

In all, this book covered twenty-five days of life-changing events that I hope will convey to you—the reader—that it's going to be okay. Yeah, things are not going to be pleasant at some points. However, we kept going, we kept loving each other, and we didn't stop believing that things would get better because they are; and they will get better. In the end, I hope they do for you too.

About the Author

Arthur was raised in Shohola, Pennsylvania. He followed his love of trucks, first becoming a truck driver, but now works in warehousing. Joyce was raised in Harding, Pennsylvania. She followed her love of music and became a music teacher. They met, fell in love, and are raising two daughters in a home they bought in Joyce's hometown.